The Lord's Supper

(Expanded Edition)

The Lord's Supper

Martin E. Marty

MINNEAPOLIS

To
Emil Hartmann
Paul Landahl
Gustav Schultz
Jack Lundin
The pastors who helped lead our children into
Christian communion

ISBN 0-8066-3339-5

The paper used in this publication meets the minimum requirements of American National Standard for Information Sciences—Permanence of Paper for Printed Library Materials, ANSI Z329.48-1984.

Manufactured in the U.S.A.   AF 9-3339

01   00   99   98   97   1   2   3   4   5   6   7   8   9   10

Contents

1. "For You . . . for Forgiveness"

LONG AGO, SO LONG AGO IN FACT that the story can include a streetcar, a pastor pulled his overcoat collar up close to his neck and ears and headed around a Boston corner into the icy northeast winds of a winter evening. Hearing a commotion, he looked up and saw a crowd gathering, despite the raw chill of the air. The people were huddling around a body that lay in agony in front of a stopped streetcar. The minister hurried over to the crumpled heap and pushed his way past the people to where a police officer and a doctor who had been passing by were tending to the injured man.

When the doctor learned that the newcomer to the scene was a priest, he said, "It's too late for me to do anything, Father! You take over. You'd better administer the last rites." The priest knew exactly what to do, even though he was barely out of seminary and had not as yet faced many emergencies. He got out his little black book and the materials he needed for the rites. Then he set out to address the writhing and now desperate man.

"My son, are you of the Catholic faith?"

"Yeah. Yeah . . ."

"Do you know that you are a sinner against God?"

"Uhuh. Yeah . . ."

The end was near. The pastor hurried along, with an eye to getting in all the words in the book.

"Do you believe in the Holy Trinity, the Father, the Son, and the Holy Ghost?"

The wretched man had just enough breath to gasp, "Say, what is this, Father? Here I am dying, and you want to run me all the way through the catechism?"

The late Richard Cardinal Cushing of Boston used to tell variations of this story about himself as that young priest. He wanted to get across a very important point that he learned through the seasoning of long years, as he got further from the books of rites and closer to the people for whom they were prepared. Last rites and Holy Communion were for dying people—which means everyone—in their daily needs. The ministry of the church has more to do with persons than with things.

Whoever has thought or studied much about the Lord's Supper knows that its story includes many things. For the man on the Boston street, these "things" would have meant being "run through the catechism." Every catechism deals with doctrines about the sacrament. Libraries are full of things called books of dogma, which define teachings about the Lord's Supper to protect it from misuse. There are other things as well, such as the many disputes that attach themselves to the means through which Jesus Christ is present among us. Most of these controversies were of the ugliest sort to be found in all the volumes about the Christian past. The Lord's Supper is also involved with things like committees and commissions, which set the rules for who should come to a meal that they all call the Lord's. More attractively, talk about the Lord's Supper includes suggestions about music appropriate to its celebration, books of direction for how to administer it, and attempts to remodel churches in order to make its impact more vivid.

Yet when sinners line up to receive the body and the blood of Jesus Christ with the earthly bread and wine— the two things that are always bound up with the act—we must picture that they have something on their minds that the literature does not address. When these believers are alert to what their very presence is shouting, if they are serious, they get right to the point: "Here I am dying—and I do not want to run through the catechism. I want to be the receiver of the gifts of God. I have the right to get to the heart, the person of Jesus Christ."

Catechisms, libraries, disputes, committees, and books of direction do have their place. Only a crude trampler of treasures from the past would kick these things aside. We inherit them and think of them as souvenirs of issues that mattered very much to the people who produced them. To pay no attention to such things is to show little regard either for our ancestors or for the deep yearnings of contemporary hearts. All the attention paid to the Lord's Supper is at least a signal that people took it very seriously and cherished something about it very much. The fact that in their choice of what to emphasize they may have erred should not deflect us from the knowledge that they "got" it—and passed it on.

The Lord's Supper is an act of God directed toward humans; it is also an act of responding humans. But an act that originated two thousand years ago at a supper in Jerusalem would have been forgotten, along with all the other suppers of that evening and of those years, if we did not have some words recording it. The earliest of these words come to us under the names of authors like Paul, Matthew, Mark, and Luke. The later words belong to people like Augustine, Teresa of Avila, John Calvin, Pope John XXIII, and Dietrich Bonhoeffer. At their worst, the later words were written to display the learning of their authors, to let them parade their egos. At their best, these words cut through side issues and become marvelously helpful for grasping the Lord's Supper.

A modern editor, William Sloane, once gave good advice to would-be writers. He claimed that when readers pick up a book (be it by William Shakespeare or Charles Dickens, or a good recent novel) they are not saying to the author, "Tell me about yourself." The writer receives no license to rattle on about eternal verities. The readers have but one thing in mind—not "tell me about you" but "tell me about me." Yes, tell me something through the characters and events you invent, but this something must make me see myself better than before and help me become a part of something greater, so that I am henceforth less personal and more human.

The catechism and stories about the Lord's Supper are of interest only when they "tell you about you." To say this is to risk playing up to one of the uglier features of modern religion. Today many people arrange the whole universe around their own egos. Some analysts say that their disease is narcissism, named after the Greek god Narcissus, who came to be literally spellbound by his own mirrored image in a pond. Narcissists can use religion, including Christianity, to become similarly spellbound. They will work every conversation around to the point that they can tell you how they were "born again." Only gradually does it become clear that some of them do this to show not how great God is but how great they are for having found God. Others will look for the latest fads or frills in the spiritual marketplace. They are saying, if they hear the story of the Lord's Supper at all, "Tell me about me." And then everything ends there.

"Tell me about me" can, however, mean something that is much better than mere self-serving. The *me* who receives the Lord's Supper is a human who in the presence of God is learning to become more human. But this meal does not merely teach; it is not a cookbook or a menu but the food itself. To share it is to experience eating and to gain its benefits. The *me* of this experience is becoming part of a larger *we* in the act of sharing the meal. The Lord's Supper is often called "Holy Communion," a coming together of bread with body, wine with blood, God with creatures, and believers with one another. To realize through Communion that one is a social human being who shares common miseries and joys is a benefit of this meal. It serves to lift a person beyond mere *me*–ness.

"Tell me about me." To prove that an accent on this notion is not just a way of catering to modern selfishness, it is necessary to look at the original records. What did the host at this meal have in mind in offering himself through it and along it? The first words of Jesus to be transmitted in writing are quoted in Paul's First Letter to the Corinthians. Before we hear anything else from Jesus' lips, we hear him saying, "This is my body which is for you." The initial act of Jesus is to overcome the distance between Jerusalem and our town, to cut across the years from his own time to ours. he clears away all the debris and clutter of secondary themes and says, "for you." That reaching out to us meets two profound demands of the heart. It shows that the speaker, who was himself near a sentence of death, knew that you do not want to run through a catechism, that you wish to be grasped and loved as a dying person. And it also meets the demands each reader makes on an author or each listener poses to a speaker; it knows that the hearers of the word of God given through Paul are saying, "Tell me about me."

"For you": The later writers and the catechisms at their best seldom fail to put this theme first. In the familiar *Small Catechism* assembled by the reformer Martin Luther, the word *you* appears three times in the combination of texts from the Bible that explain what the Lord's Supper *is*:

Our Lord Jesus on the night when he was betrayed, took bread, and when he had given thanks, he broke it, and gave it to the disciples and said, "Take, eat; this is my body which is given for *you*. Do this in remembrance of me." In the same way also he took the cup, after supper, and when he had given thanks he gave it to them, saying, "Drink of it, all of *you*. This cup is the new covenant in my blood, which is poured out for many for the forgiveness of sins. Do this, as often as *you* drink it, in remembrance of me."

In the next paragraph the catechism writer asks, "What is the benefit of such eating and drinking?" His answer: "We are told in the words 'for *you*' and 'for the forgiveness of sins.'" Let the second phrase, the matter of forgiveness, dangle for a while—we will come back to it. For the moment remember only that the "for you" with which Jesus reaches out appears in the first line that tells what the benefit is. To miss that understanding is to take the initial step on the wrong road. The road is wrong because it can never lead to the heart of Holy Communion. The Lord's Supper is not a written recipe describing how a dish called the forgiveness of sins might be prepared. Nor is it a handsome photograph from *Gourmet* magazine designed to whet appetites or to inspire criticism by connoisseurs of food. The Lord's Supper is the forgiveness of sins. It works the forgiveness of sins. The words "for you" and "for the forgiveness of sins," says Luther, "when accompanied by the bodily eating and drinking, are the chief thing in the sacrament."

The chief thing.

"FOR YOU": Through the years there have been millions of very different *you*s gathered in countless setting for this meal and its benefits. In order to break out of the confines of our own milieu, it is good to imagine another one. To do so will make possible a better understanding of the way we receive the Lord's Supper closer to our own homes. Many Christians are perfectly free to announce their gatherings in the Saturday newspapers, and by means of the bold type of billboards and church signs bid people come to these services. Therefore, let us picture a somewhat less convenient approach. A situation that might have happened in Eastern Europe provides a good example.

Because the regime in this Eastern nation opposes their faith, the Christians feel very close to each other. Partly because the government discourages them, they find a special lure in congregating. But theirs is not just the psychology of wanting the forbidden fruit. Instead, the opposition to faith helps make its meaning stand out boldly. The believers might have to do drudge work in the mines or factories that even nonmembers of the Party never have to do. In such a situation, cramped Christians live for their brief hours together. If they cannot gather daily, they will certainly cherish a weekly observance. Since meeting is so inconvenient and exciting, they arrange to save up food all week long and hold a kind of potluck supper.

While much in their country is drab, and while their own setting—perhaps a home where they will be watched less closely than in their official church build-ing—is a bit dingy, they have a spirit of joy that is vivid. They share their food in that spirit because they know that Christ has conquered, because they find each other in Christ, and because they live expecting him to return. Each person brings what he or she can to the supper. While our own churches are often defined by the income of the members who can live together in the same sub-urb, churches in the East cannot always make such dis-tinctions. An unemployed worker and a recently released prisoner will have to depend for food on whoever is better off—but who cares?

Someone has to preside at the supper. In the course of the meal, this person will hold up a loaf of bread and erupt into praise of God. To help everyone recall why God is being praised, this presider of the feast elaborates on a story which tells all those present about themselves: they are creatures, and they learn how they came to be creatures. They belong to Israel as well as to the company of the disciples, so they will want to hear their stories. These congregants are called by the name of Jesus Christ, and none of them yawns or routinely nods when the head of the feast recalls what Jesus Christ has done, is doing, and will do for them. But the presider takes special pains to recount for another week what Jesus said about this gathering. The words are those which speak of his body and blood as he took the bread and wine and gave them to the disciples in the upper room at the Last Supper.

To be sure that every *you* in the room is included, the presider will then ask whether those gathered desire to have someone or something included in the blessing. Naturally, the congregants have plenty to pray about. The unemployed person wants to praise God for the bread she receives at this Supper. It is the most food she has eaten all week. She cares for the good friends who shared the food. The ex-prisoner knows that authorities can detain him again any week. Because now he has freedom in Christ, the regime cannot tolerate him. But Jesus was with that man in prison. Christ is with him in this meal especially—and will follow him to jail or lead him to freedom tomorrow. Incredibly, given the good reasons for the worshipers to be spiteful against the regime, someone asks for prayers for the government. Not everyone can be present, because some are sick. And not everyone chooses to be present, because some do not want to risk being seen at an event on which some Christian "fifth columnist" might report; such Christians need praying for, too. Then someone remembers to give thanks for those who by their example make the others strong. By some instinct, those who contribute to the list stop before long; they are aware that unless they stop, the person at the head of the table might go on at too great length with unending words, while they want the food and drink.

So the presider, after voicing the praise, hands along the single loaf, just broken. The people thereafter hear some words about how the fragments they all hold are part of the loaf. This point is important because it renders pictorial the way the many worshipers are part of a single "loaf." They resemble the way God will finally gather the scattered fragments of his Israel.

There is a knock on the door. Everyone stops, aware that this interruption could be dangerous for the ex-prisoner, who never has been cleared in the eyes of the regime. Indeed, it could be bad for all of them. To be seen here might bring about new harassment on the job, and for the young people it could mean a limit on their education and careers. The nighttime knock has come to many before, because the people in these gatherings, while they are law-abiding, refuse to give their whole heart to the government and the Party. But this time there are relieved whispers; it is only a latecomer who wants to join in. So the participants settle back and eat. While the congregants have been hungry for food, they also welcome conversation. They talk about the little trials and joys of the day. They try to make sense of the new government restrictions and of those slight relaxations that are even harder to understand. They wonder how their distant relatives are doing, what it is like in other neighboring countries, and why, according to reports, the churches are largely empty in the West.

After a while the presider bangs on a cup, calls everyone to order, and gives a second blessing or thanksgiving—this time over a cup of wine. The people now hear more of the story of the first Lord's Supper. Suddenly the pleasant chatter has ended and they talk of the sacred center of their faith. These Christians think of the way

Jesus went from this Supper to trial and death. The presider moves things along by sipping from the cup and passing it around for others to drink. The meal ends rather abruptly, as people gather their boxes and baskets. They pick up the leftovers, since it will be a week before they eat this well again. They also take along each other's greetings, since they cannot count on soon again being in the company of people who share their hopes. The parting guests carry with them a sense of the blessing of God. If anyone should run up to them tonight and ask whether they have "met the Lord" or "received Jesus Christ," each would have an answer: "Yes, the Lord came in his Supper and I received him." Such persons would have caught the main point: This event and its gift are "for you."

This description, appropriate as it is for the church living under the cross, carries us a very long distance from the way in which the Lord's Supper got started. Or does it? Translate "regime" into "empire," or "eastern Europe" into "Rome," and you will have not the story of a modern secret meal but a pieced-together version of what the earliest Lord's Suppers evidently were like after the resurrection of Jesus. This version relies on what is known from Jewish practice, the new Testament narrative of the upper room, and the earliest nonbiblical records of the meal.

Our composite version does not settle everything we want to know about early gatherings for the Lord's Supper. All the biblical accounts, except one in the Fourth Gospel, connect the meal with the Jewish Passover, so it is natural to think of the meal in that light. In every case, pious Jews—which is what the early Christians were— would always break their bread with a great blessing and with praise to God. Their host would share the first piece of food with the guests. At any special meal they would end by sharing a cup of wine and giving thanks. When the Christians later moved away from the Jewish world, these elements, which were taken for granted, would have disappeared had not Paul and others taken pains to pass them on. But the non-Jewish world brought other threats to the sacred gathering. Pagan customs confused the participants in these holy acts. That is why most Christians eventually separated their ordinary meal from the sacred or sacramental event. The New Testament writings tell of the abuses that led them to make such a painful separation. It is likely that Christians did continue having the meal together, even if they did so in a different room or made a clear breach before they moved on to the sacrament.

By setting the Lord's Supper in Eastern Europe and then revisiting it back in early Christianity, we can see how portable it is and how transportable its meanings are. Sometimes you will hear people insist that because they enjoy an extremely simple order of service theirs is closest in form and spirit to the earliest Lord's Suppers. Their impulse is understandable. Martin Luther shared it when he said, "Doubtless our mass will be the better, the closer it is to the mass of Christ; and the more precarious, the farther it is from the same." That is a good rule, but Luther himself could not follow it. For example, he used the word *mass*, which early Christians did not use. It came from a Latin word that told believers the rite was over.

If being close to the mass of Christ is the goal, it can be very complicated. If the Last Supper was indeed a Passover meal, it was anything but simple, as anyone can testify who has ever attended a Jewish Seder. To be close to the mass of Christ means that we could be sure of our achievement only if we restricted the meal to thirteen Jewish men in an upper room. Being close to the mass of Christ has to mean something different from literal imitating of the external circumstances of the first meal or meals.

WE ARE ALL WORLDS AWAY from early Christianity, and most of us are far from Eastern Europe. Many experimental communities in Western Christianity today are not content with what they believe are routine repetitions of the Lord's Supper. Some of them have done research into the nature of Jewish worship and have used their findings to inform their practice of the Christian sacrament. Some communes of modern Christians share a Lord's Supper which, because they connect it with a common meal, provides a more nearly exact reenactment. But the vast majority of people are not interested in stories that reconstruct ancient worship unless those stories satisfy their demand to "Tell me about me." The believers will be respectful of research, but their final goal will be to realize the words "for you," and to know that with their bodily eating and drinking they receive the body and blood of a present Christ.

Rather than dwell on the experimental or exotic, we will find it more valuable to observe a day in the life of a modern communicant, a believer who partakes of the Lord's Supper. To be interested only in historical discovery would be "running through the catechism" when we want instead to discover hungry, dying, living, joyful, hoping persons and congregations. We are likely to find that behind the ordinary divine service are extraordinary meanings. What at first seems trivial turns out to tell us much about ourselves.

I am going to trace the day and its meaning by following a character. All such characters need names. This one we shall call *you*. If one reader welcomes personal writing that demands the second-person *you*, this device will be congenial. If another reader likes to retain bit of distance from the writer and the story, picturing *you* as a character with whom to compare and contrast oneself will do almost as well. Since there are many kinds of *you*s in the Christian church, we shall have to do some imagining, fully aware that this character is not typical, average, or entirely representative. You may not have a spouse or a family or a church building like those of the *you* in these pages. But you can feel enough at home with the emotions and practices of other *you*s to pursue the character's encounter with the meanings of the Lord's Supper.

2. Preparation

YOU AWAKEN TO AN INSISTENT ALARM CLOCK. After waiting a moment, you pound it into submissive silence and roll over—only to rouse yourself with a dim recall that you were supposed to get up. Why did you commit yourself to early service today? The party ran late last night, and you feel dragged back to the pillow. But you hear stirring. You get up, dress, and meet the family. Breakfast is slight; you will be brunching after a while anyway. Besides, you all agreed to get your own meager fare or do without breakfast entirely on Sundays before church. So the family gathers and sits, heads bowed, and you say to the youngest, "Now follow me. Do what I do. 'God be in my head. God be in my heart. God be on the left of me. God be on the right of me.'" You have just helped a member of a new generation learn the sign of the cross. That lesson is in a way "running her through the catechism" because it was from the catechism that you first learned what you later neglected to practice— until you married a formerly Roman Catholic spouse who retaught you its meaning. Martin Luther gave you a formula: "In the morning, when you rise, make the sign of the cross and say, 'In the name of God, the Father, the Son, and the Holy Spirit. Amen.'"

You did not feel at home with the sign of the cross as the first mark of the day because it seemed at best magical and at worst unimportant—magical because you were once turned off to see basketball players make the sign at the free-throw line, as if by some incantation they could cause God to make the ball fall through the hoop. The sign also seemed unimportant, a mere gesture— like kneeling or standing, bowing your head, or folding your hands. Yet if you thought about its meaning as you made it, you will have just participated in one of the two most radical acts of your day, the other being the receiving in faith of the body and blood of Christ.

What is so radical about the sign of the cross? It is neither magical nor unimportant, but a reminder of what you will see later today during a baptism. Remember: "Child of God, you have been sealed by the Holy Spirit and marked with the cross of Christ forever." Meanwhile, "the minister marks the sign of the cross on the forehead of the baptized." When you make that sign at the beginning of the day, the sign itself does not do anything the way baptism does things. It does not identify you with Christ and make a new person out of you. But the sign of the cross reminds you of this identify. It helps you imagine your situation. You repent, which means that you turn yourself around 180 degrees, so that your old self is left behind. Then God works the act of making you new in Christ. That theme appears also in the writings of Paul (Romans 6:4) and in the catechism of Luther: The new person "should come forth daily and rise up, cleansed and righteous, to live forever in God's presence."

Maybe not all those thoughts crossed your mind as you made the sign of the cross. Maybe you had different thoughts from last week or from yesterday. You were, in any case, preparing yourself for this day, the Lord's Day and the Lord's Supper day. If someone should ask you later today, "Are you born again?" You could answer, "Yes, on _____ ," and fill in the date of your baptism. If such a reply is unsatisfactory to the questioner (since you may have been a sleeping child at that time) and the question is repeated, "Are you born again?", you can answer, "Yes, this morning , at 7:30 A.M., when I returned to my baptism."

With the sign of the cross marking your day, maybe you sip a bit of juice or coffee and taste some toast; maybe you don't. The work *breakfast* means that you are breaking your fast, your overnight time without food. But many Christians choose not to break fast until they receive the bread and wine of the Lord's meal. No one is supposed to receive brownie points or merit badges for fasting, making the sign of the cross, or any other mode of bodily preparation. But we are learning more each year about how closely our bodies and spirits are interlocked and interactive. For centuries many Christians were not allowed to eat or even drink water after midnight, before communing. In reaction, their heirs and other Christians kicked over all traces of such practices. It is often non-Christians who are again teaching church people that one can clear the mind, be open to new experiences, and be ready for the deep things of life by generating a positive hunger. If you do not want to follow that severe a discipline, "going light" is at least a reminder. And not opening the Sunday paper at this hour is also a creative way to keep the mind and spirit uncluttered and open.

You make your way to a house of God. You have sensed something special about this day, the Lord's Day. You have resisted the impulse of many modern people to flatten it out with all the other six. You can, of course, commune on Holy Thursday or on a Saturday morning at a retreat. But there is a freshness about Sunday that makes it possible for you to easily identify with early Christians who, as far as we can tell, turned "the Eighth Day," the "festival of light," into a weekly observance of the Lord's presence in this meal. You are with him, though his presence and form are unrecognized until he causes your heart to burn within you while he talks to you and while he opens to you the Scriptures, as once he did with two disciples on the post-Easter road outside Emmaus. And on Sunday you are there with him again, at an Emmaus nearer home. You recall how in the evening when at table, he took the bread, blessed and broke it, and gave it to the

two disciples, and how their eyes were opened; they recognized him and told others "how he was known to them
in the breaking of the bread." Whatever else is down the
road for you this Sunday, you will first have your eyes
opened and you will recognize him when he breaks the
bread "for you."

Your mind could be full of many things by this time of
the morning. They could all seem contradictory; this is
called a supper, yet you enjoy it at breakfast time. Some
call it the eucharist or thanksgiving, a festival of joy, but
you will see many dreary and glum faces as people come
from the table. This is a banquet of unity among
Christians, yet nothing divides Christian churches more.
It grows from the simple act of Jesus giving himself, and
yet it has inspired the most complicated of Christian doctrines. It is the *Lord*'s Supper, yet humans make it look as
if they are the inviters, or those who dare bar the door.
Christ gave it for the sake of love, yet people fall into pettiness of conflict over its meanings. Well-informed and
well-intentioned leaders do what they can to grasp the
biblical and historical purposes. Hoping to help bring you
into the recalled company of saints who went before, they
use a language intended to prepare you for the other six
days of the week, only to find that many church members
dispute almost everything they write or speak.

If your mind is full of these things, it only shows that
you are human. The old person that you were lives on
in you in spite of the sign of the cross and your return to
baptism. Your mind is not clear and focused, even if you
did fast. The grayness of dark days, many of them caused
by Christian clouds, hangs over you. What matters is that
you do not let it get you down. You are going to church,
where a story will "tell you about you" and where an act
will make it possible for God to be there "for you."
Everything else is secondary, and you know it. You have
your priorities right. You have thought about what you

wear this day, about gas gauges and stoplights, about what you have planned for the afternoon. But you have not thought chiefly about such things. And you have not let yesterday haunt you with guilt, or tomorrow nag you with worry. You are free for what is to go on joining the gathered congregation on the other side of the door.

You find yourself barely on time, which means later than you wanted to be, so you duck into a back seat. That seems to be safe because it keeps you far from the action. You will not feel emotionally close to what is going on. Several rows separate you from the next worshipers, so there is no hazard that you will need to feel like part of a congregation. By your position you are sending out a little message that says, "I am a very private person and want to remain that way. I am here, but I don't want to be bothered."

Then a second thought hits you. If you have an interest in having your mass be closer to the mass of Christ, you might do what you would have done in the upper room or the living room long ago, or in the little hall in Eastern Europe. So you move into the zone of action, where your senses will be alert. The logic of your choice to relocate affects you strangely. You feel a little warming in your ears. You blush to think how for so long you had been doing everything possible to dim the sense of the presence of God and to keep the congregation remote. It's not that something magical is going on here, something that works better at close range. The word of God can work also at the fringes. Forgiveness is "for you" even if you hunch apathetically back there in the shadows. But, front or center, you now have new opportunities to take part.

The little folder you hold announces that today the service of Holy Communion begins with a "Brief Order for Confession and Forgiveness." It need not, and it does not always do so. Christ's mass did not include it, and you want your mass to be like his. The mass of the earliest Christians, so far as we know, did not begin with such a formula. But it may be true that "what is everybody's job is nobody's job" and that the confession no one makes provision for may never happen. With your prayer and the sign of the cross each morning, you should be examining yourself. You have confessed and have been forgiven already this morning, perhaps even at the special service. You are not to get the idea that the congregation must gather for this special conversation with God in order to round out the Lord's Supper and thus make it effective. Today, however, the little order is here, and you do confess.

In the middle of these lines reposes one that is easy to overlook. It calls for "silence for reflection and self-examination." Silence is an important element in worship. These days people are learning once again to be drawn nearer to God with the help of devices that eliminate sounds. You try this one, but your mind wanders. In the silence, you hear someone else's stomach rumble; you are tempted to be embarrassed, but the little noise does not distract anyone else. A child whimpers or laughs for a moment, but you imagine that in early Christianity or at that early Eastern European potluck supper that children were restless, too. Meditate! Suddenly your mind fills with images: of transcendental meditators and their gurus; of the hippies and their masters long ago; of Christian mystics who employed meditation to climb their ladder ever so wearily to the presence of God; of . . . When is the minute going to end? Isn't the minister letting it go on too long?

Then, so slowly and subtly that you hardly realize it, you find a space clearing in your mind and heart. The call is for self-examination; in silence you find what the stir of the world never did permit. The examination becomes very concrete. You do not like everything you found in the recesses of the mind and heart. You are thinking now not of pettiness in general but of the way you withheld your love from a spouse or child. You recall not lust in general but the way you lust for money and arrange all your life to get it. You look forward to expressing hate, but not in a battlefield against the enemies of Christ; no, you wait instead to get in your licks against the head of another congregational faction at the next meeting. You think of what party-spirit means and realize that you shared it when you wanted to define the only right way of settling on something in the Christian life—even though countless reliable Christians chose another way.

In the confession today you find once again that the Lord's presence is not dependent on your virtuosity at locating more sins than anyone else. This is not a contest among the connoisseurs of confession to see who can proclaim, "We're number one!" Who cares who can grovel most gracelessly or boast a naturally more restrained emotional outlook? You are not supposed to be in the business of "Hey! Look at me, God! I am chief of sinners!" This is not the means of preparing for the best kind of Communion. You do not have to worry about whether you feel badly enough about yourself. In the New Testament, repenting is often a joyful act of people who are enabled to prepare the way of the Lord. They are the members of the bridal party. What they have in common is not a personality type or a technique for confessing but a sense of need and an awareness that God is addressing them to make them new. Some days, it is true, you *have* sat there succumbing to a sense of torture or guilt. But today you are not sorry that you are not sorry in that way. Sometimes you join the weary climbers, but on other days you merely shoot a figurative stab at the loving heart of God. Most frequently, in the silence you are full of a quiet resolve to listen, to receive what God offers.

DURING THE INTERIM between that brief order of confession and the beginning of Holy Communion, you have time to focus your thoughts. Typically, Christians find themselves thinking about their involvement in the Lord's Supper.

You may ask, for example, how frequently should my congregation and I being doing this? It would be dishonest to claim that all Christians in history have communed weekly. In medieval Catholicism a parish might have had fifty masses per week, buy many of them occurred with no congregation present. Some believers took part only once a year, at Christmas or Easter. Their approach is not a model for anyone, including today's Roman Catholics. Some church bodies make provisions only for annual or quarterly Communions. They have come a long way from what we surmise was the biblical and early Christian pattern. Believers at that time, it seems, seldom came together without breaking fast and receiving Christ in this meal and form. There have been times when Christians of some parties thought it best to go infrequently: that way they could store up sins to be forgiven. Meanwhile they went on their own as long as possible, so that when God finally did reach them in the Lord's Supper it "would not seem routine." Today some congregations celebrate infrequently because they think Communion prolongs the service, though it need not. The sacrament might cut in on a forty-five minute sermon, only fifteen minutes of which contemporary mortals could have stayed with anyhow. More and more it is becoming less and less controversial to recover earlier practices and to make the Lord's Supper available weekly in at least one service at each place where Christians who believe in Christ's presence gather.

On another Sunday, you might focus on such thoughts as: Just what are we doing here? What is going on? Why have a meal in a ritual setting? Why do practical-minded modern people trek to a place where they do things like kneeling? Here, persons wearing robes that they would not dare be seen in elsewhere take a bit of bread and put it into the hands of worshipers. Then they offer them wine from a cup. The cup may be a common chalice, as it certainly was in the Jewish and early Christian gatherings. If you are alert to issues of hygiene, you might find your reverie momentarily reinterrupted at this point, but soon you re back to the flow of other questions. Why are grown people singing here? Why do we do this more or less the same way every week? Why the relative formality?

The organ will be the fourth part of a fugue by the time you sort out all these questions. But it is creative now and then to picture yourself as an anthropologist, a student of primitive cultures who stumbles upon you and your fellows. This scholar will ask, "What do these tribal rites mean?" You can ask such questions without reducing them Lord's Supper to nothing but a rite. "Nothing buttery" would be a way of saying that no special meanings can come with a ritual. But to avoid anthropologists' questions entirely is to refuse having some light shed on your practices.

Thus you can play the neutral scholar long enough to reflect on why you are enjoying a meal in a sacred setting. Experts will tell you that, second only to the sexual union of a faithful married pair, no human activity is as intimate and bonding as a meal. You understood that perfectly at the time you started dating the person who became your spouse. When the two of you turned really serious, you shared an elaborate and possibly expensive meal. Couples turn anniversaries into events by revisiting a special restaurant, or silver or golden anniversaries into occasions by inviting in the the clan. You yourself had a wedding supper to help seal your joy, just as people at Cana in Galilee did when they invited in Jesus Christ. You might strike a business deal over lunch. You do this not simply because you have to eat anyhow and can deduct it from your taxes but because the deal takes on more significance at a meal. After a graveside rite, someone invited you in for a cup of coffee and some cold cuts. You then affirmed in different words the risen life of one you just heard celebrated by a person who held a little black book at the graveside. You host weekend guests, and you and they drift and wander around the house. But when you gather over the candles at a well-prepared meal, you focus your intimacies, your memories and hopes.

If you ever took out a red pencil and chose to underline all the times the biblical story told you about you, you were probably astonished to see how often people experienced divine visitations over a meal. Three visitors came to Abraham, and he prepared a meal. The children of Israel were to come out of bondage, and they ate a Passover feast. Jesus wanted to associate with outcasts and sinners and, however shocking to others, he signaled his identity with them by sitting with them at table. It is that history which Jesus interrupted and to which he added when, on "the night in which he was betrayed," he kept with his disciples at this most sacred meal.

Next to you is someone whose random thoughts may come together around the questions "Why are we congregating?" and "Why can't Christians have a full spiritual life without coming here for this meal?" They believe that God is everywhere. Individuals come into contact with God in the silence of their bedrooms, in the noise of the trenches, in the hours of any humdrum day. Everywhere around them people are sending out signals which suggest that being alone or one-on-one is enough. Christians may listen to religious radio programs or watch Christian television shows for a year and never once be encouraged to congregate for the Lord's Supper. No one will ever tell them that there was a sacred meal and that there is one now. The airport bookstore peddles fifty ways to find, experience, or feel good about God— but hardly ever will one page in its books point to this central Christian way of knowing the presence of God, this meal in the midst of a congregation.

Without realizing it, you have found it easy to drift into this pattern of rotation. When you were in the hospital you eavesdropped on a broadcast church service or tuned in to an entertaining Christian television speaker. That's when you began this meandering. You did not realize at first that while fascinating speakers were scolding about the evils of the United States, they never once caused you to search your heart, as your preacher will today. If the media evangelists would hit too close to home, you could simply change the channel. No matter what they do, they cannot make a real congregation out of you. Your connection with them is limited to the electronic waves they employ and the mail you use in responding with a financial contribution. You are part of a clientele or a cause, but never a congregation. No sister or brother can go up to you and ask, "Do you realize that this time you've gone too far to be reached, or to help?" And you reach out for help. No one can say, "This burden is too heavy for me; can you grab some of it?" Whatever good these isolated spiritual teachers did when you were in spiritual isolation, you keep feeling a hunger for Christ and his company. You realized that "to be" is "to be together," for the sake of all humanity and for many kinds of spirituality. You relearned the biblical theme that Jesus Christ exists *as* and not merely *in* congregation, for he is the head of a body whose members have to be together, not just in theory but also in action. And when you caught on to that, it was little wonder that you wanted to congregate with others to hear the Word and to share this event.

Debates over the frequency of the Lord's Supper, scholarly talk about the function of rites and meals, and reflections on congregating, however, are not the chief thing. Only belief in the "for you" and "for the forgiveness of sins," accompanied by the bodily eating and drinking, is vital. Philosopher William James once urged readers to seek the "commanding vision" of an author so that everything else will fall into place. "For you . . . for forgiveness" is the commanding vision in this understanding of the Lord's Supper; everything else follows from it. Lose sight of it and the meal will become merely a nice rite. Einar Billing, a Swedish Christian leader, has suggested that we picture a system of Christian thought not as a collection of doctrines set like pearls on a string but as a glowing core, with everything else taking light and warmth from the center, like the rays from the sun. The glowing core of this meal is "for you . . . for forgiveness," and all the other rays emerge from it.

3. The Service

THE MINISTERS ENTER. They may be following a cross, which now is a sign above the bodies of the whole baptized congregation. Those who follow it signal their awareness that they have been reborn today. This cross represents the call to discipleship, to the fellowship of Christ's suffering. There may be some candle lighting and movement by a choir. If there is a procession, it exists chiefly to help you separate your thinking from those reveries that went before and the distractions of a gray or jarringly busy world around you. The movement states that something special is going on here. But do not be fooled. That cross may be made of gold, but it should shock you as much as if they were wheeling into position an electric chair, gallows, or a guillotine. Those candles may create glistening auras and halos; you remember how as a child you half shut your eyes and almost saw angelic light around them.

But candles also pierced the darkness for ancient congregants back when the Christians worshiped in catacombs, or in your century when they needed a flaming wick to provide meager light over smuggled bread and wine in a concentration camp. Christians have often gathered for this meal in secret rooms, behind closed doors where a procession with trumpets would only have attracted the notice of the authorities. If these features underscore the "for you, for forgiveness," well and good; let them all be splendid. The week ahead will be drab enough.

Next everyone sings a hymn, perhaps a psalm. Adults may not join voices again all week, unless perhaps to mumble their way through the national anthem at an athletic event. But this singing is different; that is clear from the very outset. The words of the ENTRANCE HYMN* itself reinforce the idea that what follows is to involve you in the blessing and peace of God. These lines then tell you about you more than do many mawkish spiritual songs which give God a full report on your passing emotions. "THE GRACE of our Lord Jesus Christ . . . be with you"— the "president" or minister up front speaks the greeting, and you respond. The brief exchange between pastor and people is a serious conversation which implies a true partnership.

With Christians of all ages you soon find yourself praying the KYRIE prayers for the peace from above; clearly that peace is "for you." Then you ask for the peace of the world and the well-being of the church, though you may wince to think how little well-being and unity you have ever seen in the churches you have known. Lord have mercy! You find yourself joining in a song that takes its first measures from the angelic announcement on the night of Jesus' birth: "Glory to God in the highest, and peace to his people on earth." These words also lift far above the reportorial earthbound hymns, and they too tell you about you because they give glory to the God who sustains you. You may instead find yourself singing words that take off from the event of Easter, "the feast of victory for our God." These words remember the Lamb whose "blood set us free to be people of God." A congregation cannot get much closer in song to the commanding vision of "for you . . . for forgiveness." Nothing has happened yet this morning to cloud that vision with its glowing core. Even the PRAYER OF THE DAY spoken on this particularly Sunday maintains the focus. And you pray too, making the leader's words your own.

* The capitalized words identify features of the liturgy in the *Lutheran Book of Worship*. Other evangelically catholic orders of service will be very similar.

Then, whether in Eastern Europe or in North America, among the rich or the poor, the reverent or the distracted, on a Sunday morning you find yourself listening to three readings from scriptures that are two or three thousand years old. Because you hear LESSONS like these every week, you find it hard to understand how peculiar, even how shocking, this simple part of the Lord's Supper is. The church which provided the readings, the readers, and the listeners seems to assume that these stories, too, are "for you."

How can words "do" something? That they are indeed supposed to do something is suggested by the next line of the catechism paragraph we began quoting above (about the benefit "for you"): "By these words the forgiveness of sins, life, and salvation are given to us in the sacrament, for where there is forgiveness of sins, there are also life and salvation." Not all the words in the ancient lessons we hear every week directly offer forgiveness. Some of them thunder the judgment of God and accuse the congregation; others are stories depicting forgiveness. But when they come to their overall point, they signal the activity of a God who works "for you," to make you new and acceptable. Words *do* this. For the congregation such words are not mere words; they become instruments, tools, and agents.

The strangeness of this practice of reading from Scripture still haunts you. The words do not come from ancient Greek or Roman histories. The congregation is not a Shakespeare society that meets to dissect the playwright's terms and phrases, nor is it a Robert Burns memorial society that gathers to recall a poet. Neither is the congregation a collection of keepers of the city of the dead, people who come to hear about the way their club is a custodian of burial plots, including one of a dead Christ. Rather these are stories from the people of Israel and the new people of God. They are told "for you," and thenceforth they become your story.

That a story can save, as can a meal, is remarkable, but we know very little about how and why stories save. As you did with the meal, ask what part stories play in ordinary life. When someone becomes important to you, you begin to tell each other the story of your life. To share with someone the story of your day makes you part of each other's ways. If you invest in a firm, you need to hear about the company's performance, even if this be in the form of a comparative financial statement. In elementary school, children hear the story of their country; elders hope that it will attract the loyalty of a new generation. In a tribe, the young ones hear the myths that bind the people together. Not all these various kinds of stories can be stories "for you," but the biblical record is "for you." Because its commanding vision is the movement of God toward a historical people, not all its parts have to fit neatly together. The story unfolds among unlikely people in a world far away. Yet the believer does not stand *outside* the story. The Bible has a plot, and you are *in* it. At Holy Communion these ancient readings serve to help develop that plot and draw together the people in it. Those who hear will therefore have more in common at the subsequent meal. Without the story, they will forget, and that will make them less human. The story describes the action of God. It works faith. It heals. The Lord's Supper will make the words visible.

While you might have heard a number of different readers, some of which were from the congregation, you now turn your attention to a minister who stands behind a book, reads from it, and if you are fortunate, declares its truth "for you." If you are unfortunate, you will get a book review, a comment on world affairs, some how-to advice for personal success, or some doctrinal comment about the word. A good homily or SERMON relentlessly plumbs a text and lets its depths reach you. It speaks to the baptized people of God, God's new people, or invites those present to join the baptized. Such a sermon points to the forthcoming meal. After a bad sermon the meal has to do the work all on its own.

In the Lord's Supper, the act of preaching adds to the general sense of strangeness. The preacher may use bad grammar and have some annoying mannerisms that make you wish you had stayed in the back pew. Preachers themselves sometimes embody even bad ways of life, about which you know just enough to let yourself be distracted from what is being said. Some preachers' opinions may be shaky and their proclamations wrong. Preachers are fallible, but this meal is also for them and for their forgiveness, including forgiveness for sins they may demonstrate in the very act of preaching. And yet we call what they are doing "preaching the word of God." Insofar as they stick to the story of the mighty deeds of God, the love of God in Jesus Christ, and the power of the Holy Spirit who is at work in presenting the story through the Scriptures, this is divine Word.

For Martin Luther, the church is not a "feather house" for quill pens, like a secretarial office or a library; it is a "mouth house." The word is not so much *geschrieben* ("written") as it is *geschrieen* ("shouted"). In preaching, when the spoken word comes to the assembled congregation, something really happens—it does not *not* happen—God is present.

Someone asks, "Have you met the Lord today?"

"Yes," you say, "in the stumbling words of a laborious preacher."

"Are you born again?"

"Yes," you reply, "in response to the word that works faith in me, leading me to leave behind 'the old self.'"

The words of the Scripture readings and the sermon are great spellings-out of the very few words in the four narratives through which the Bible details the first Lord's Supper. We think of them as part of the response to a catechism question, "How can bodily eating and drinking produce such great effects?" Be archaic for a moment and listen to the old-fashioned but startling answer:

> The eating and drinking do not in themselves produce the effects, but the words "for you" and "for the forgiveness of sins." These words, when accompanied by the bodily eating and drinking, are the chief thing in the sacrament, and anyone who believes these words has what they say and declare: the forgiveness of sins.

Here are perfectly blended and held together the two basic features of the Christian sacrament—words and elements, both received in faith. To talk about which is prime or prior is idle at this point. Debating about whether the pulpit for preaching or the table for the Supper should have architectural dominance is futile. At the Lord's Supper they are put together, and no human should put them asunder. THE HYMN OF THE DAY is a response and a reinforcement of both.

The person who believes has what the words offer. Faith or belief is still another integral element in the Lord's Supper. The congregants are to cling to the words in faith and to receive the bread and wine in faith. This means that they are to be serious people; God is making signs toward them. For them to fail to discern these signs and thus remain in unbelief is something for which they are held responsible. Jesus often berated people for their unbelief. This does not mean that he attacked atheists or agnostics. He did not spend time criticizing people who could not spit back all the appropriate intellectual answers to the catechism questions of his day. The unbelievers he scolded were usually the religious people of the day who could not recognize how God was present in Christ. More often he chided his own disciples. Their unbelief led them to overlook the meaning of his words and his work among them, because they were constantly attempting to evade the cross and they wanted Jesus to escape it as well.

Unbelief would not let God be God. Unbelief would not let God choose to work through Jesus of Nazareth. Lack of faith was visible when people with empty lives tried to fill them with efforts to impress God: "Look, Lord, how'm I doing?" Jesus chose to praise faith among the simple folk who came to him, people who were not part of the historic people of God. These "little ones" were open to the healing he could give. These outsiders were the chief models for belief, as were the tax collectors, prostitutes, and poor people who had no place but to him to go to for acceptance. Many of these outsiders became insiders. After his disciples saw Jesus risen from the dead, they too began to recognize him, especially "in the breaking of the bread." In the course of time the believers began to make a group response of faith, a CREED. Some of these responses were as short as "Jesus is Lord!"

In the course of centuries, certain formulas of faith developed, among them the Nicene Creed and the Apostles' Creed. In formal worship today most Christians include one or the other in the Lord's Supper, though nothing like them was uttered in the upper room at the first such meal. More likely, especially if that first Supper was a Passover meal, the disciples present heard stories instead of reciting creeds. But while believers do not regard these formulas as having dropped from heaven or as being necessary for Holy Communion, they take delight in "confessing" them. This means that the worshipers stand up before God, each other, and the world and boldly speak their faith in God. They give voice to their commanding vision.

In some service books the *Credo* ("I believe") of the Nicene Creed is translated "we believe"—in order to bring out the way Jesus Christ exists as congregation. The plural formulation stresses how the members share one faith as the limbs share one body. The Apostles' Creed is more personal: "I believe . . ." We should probably think "I" when saying "we," and think "we" when saying "I," for here as so often in the Holy Communion we have to hold together two ideas that could easily be in tension or even fall apart.

The "for you" of the Lord's Supper is spoken to the whole congregation of the faithful and to each member personally. As the early accounts tell it, Jesus did not interrupt the common meal which was uniting the people and say anything like:

> Bartholomew, over there in the back corner, you have nothing in common with anyone else around. I saw your "I Found It!" bumper sticker telling me that you had fulfilled your quest. You have been telling everyone that you have decided for me as your personal Savior. That's good, and to recognize that, let me leave the pack and break a piece of bread off "for you." Now you can go home.

Nor did Jesus say:

> I don't care much about people. I came not to save the individual but to save the whole world. Mine is to be a mass movement, and such movements are made up of masses, not persons. If I have to stop for each one of you, how can I make the rounds of all? I have come to save humanity. It is humans I have no time for.

Both statements are inconceivable. People today make too sharp a distinction between belief in and through a people and belief on one's own or doing one's own thing in one's own way. In the biblical sweep, God is always saving a people. Once, we hear, Israel was not a people, but now it is a people. Not to belong to a people was a great horror. And yet within that people very vivid personalities stood out. A modern novelist can take four verses or four chapters of the Old Testament and write four volumes of fiction based on them, as Thomas Mann did with the figure of Joseph. These ancient people were secure in their identity. As members of a people they knew who they were. They had more individuality than many people in the era of computers, people who go to extremes to have everything "custom designed" and "personally styled" so that they can stand out.

The God who is saving a congregation also saves people. The "for you" is for *each* of you, in your marvelous particularities. You, the alcoholic rising above your demon, and you, the suddenly unemployed mid-career executive. You, the proud parents of a newly baptized child, and you, the Peruvian peasant whose public life has seen none of the liberation that God would work among the people. You, the half-awake worshiper, and you, the alert one. You, the one who has doubts that this word and this meal will help overcome, and you who, having taken pains to think through all the dogma, sometimes think you know more about God than God does. Most of all, you who now gain confidence to express faith by reciting a creed full of astonishing statements like "We acknowledge one Baptism for the forgiveness of sins. We look for the resurrection of the dead, and the life of the world to come." The moment you said those opening words, "We believe in one God," you set yourself up for those last words as well. Or is God to *stop* loving in the presence of death?

Neither creed in its articulation of faith directly uses the words that accompany the eating and drinking in the Lord's Supper, but all the words of both creeds address the commanding vision, the core of faith out of which all the rest flows. The Nicene Creed, especially when it speaks of Jesus Christ, becomes direct: *"For us* and for our salvation he came down from heaven; . . . *For our sake* he was crucified. . . ."￼ On some days the congregation will utter these words along with the act of Baptism. On some days the people may not speak them at all. All life is to be an act of confession. Different words—in sermons, hymns, and prayers—can equally reinforce the response of a people.

If all members of a congregation can keep the "we" and the "I" of the creeds together, they will be prepared for those desperate moments when they will seem to be on their own. It has been said that just as one must believe for oneself, so one must die for oneself. Even if we are surrounded by our family and friends, our dying is the ultimately lonely act. Here the "for you" of personal faith is the strongest assurance of the divine presence. On such a day a messenger from the congregation may bring to you the food and drink of the Lord's Supper because you had to be away when the congregation gathered. This messenger will also bring words of encouragement and comfort. But there will also be a need for leave-taking. For that journey, this is the food; and to prepare for it, this faith is the road map. Yet it is also wrong to speak of our dying completely alone. Only Jesus had to utter a cry of abandonment, a shout that signaled how separated and alone he was. But God vindicated Jesus, and from that time on we die without being abandoned or alone. We die in company, as the Lord's Supper makes clear when it joins us with all who have gone before. We believe. I believe.

THE PRAYERS normally follow the creed. These can include intercession. Intercession is loving your neighbor on your knees. While prayer for others was natural for those early Christians, or for the huddled faithful in Eastern Europe, at their best they took comfort in the fact that they were members of a church that went far beyond their own locale. So today the prayers are a place wherein Christians commit themselves to the good of the whole church and world, and their lives to action for the sake of that good.

Well into the Lord's Day, you suddenly detect a shift in the character of your observance. Despite all the talk about eating, up to this point it has been only that—talk. Up to this point you have heard descriptions, prescriptions, and recipes, though admittedly these give life in their own way. But a meal is an activity. And this week you decide to take special note of its movements. On one level, what follows is like a very slow dance, choreographed to match solemn moments. Behind much liturgy is the dance, a sign that people recognize how God wants us to enjoy the divine presence. The people have their steps to take, as do their leaders. God works through gestures as God works through our words; we are asked to yield our bodies, and here is a chance to do just that.

In a pattern that recalls the earliest Communion, the minister offers the PEACE to the people. Then they may share it with each other. The former peace is spoken and embarrasses no one; it is easy to let it slide by unheard. The latter is gestured, and either upsets or thrills most people. The passing of the peace can take the pattern of rather formal hand greetings or more personal embraces. With it people speak a formula, such as "the peace of Christ be with you," or some personally applied words of greeting. A member near you is just back from the hospital; surely you will mention that in the peace, as the minister does in the prayer. Whatever occurs between members, it should be as natural as possible, in order to recall the living-room character of early Christian worship, and not be so compulsive as to disrupt the flow and tone of the whole service.

Why does something that calls for motion of the body elicit every kind of sarcasm and ribaldry from nervous Christians? The New Testament writings are emphatic about the exchange of greetings and kisses of peace among believers. Yet when contemporary conservative liturgists set out to reach further back in the tradition to restore what later ages forgot, traditionalists began to sniff and snort in reaction against such "modern" tamperings. They resorted to every kind of colorful and putting-off phrase in order to attack the idea that Christian people should pass the peace of Christ to each other. You know, of course, that it is important to respect individual differences, and you need not expect the same kind of enthusiasm from everyone. But once you saw how the gestures of peace embodied a sense of the "for you" of the Lord's Supper, how they brought people into a vivid sense of union, you began to overcome your own reserve and to bear the burdens and share the joys of others. The peace is not the chief thing in the sacrament, by any means. Nor is it necessary for guests to greet one another when they come together for a meal in someone's house. They will receive the same number of calories with or without greetings.

While the whole motion of the Lord's Supper is toward you, it also includes pledges in return, called responses. These come to a climax in an OFFERTORY. Long ago, at the first Lord's Supper, Jesus and the disciples made provision for the meal itself. Today people offer not only bread and wine but other gifts which they want to give to God for God's work. Evangelical Christians once necessarily fought off the idea that the Lord's Supper was an achievement of their own. They dared not let it be a sacrifice designed to impress God, to tie God down to various obligations. They therefore began to underplay and even to negate responses. All the figurative arrows symbolizing direction came from heaven above to the earthly table, and from the sacred table to the sinful people.

If somewhere in the Christian world rearguard actions in that battle are still necessary, let the people beware of the Offertory. But battle lines change through the centuries. One critic said that he had gone to many churches and heard the preacher say, "Don't try to impress God with your works" or "Don't try to keep the rules and regulations and thus win your way." He looked around at nearly slumbering collections of utterly casual Christians and wondered, "Who's trying?"

The privilege of offering bread and wine, which are human reworkings of the divine gifts, and of bringing money to stand for other forms of earthly goods, is far too rich to be pushed aside because some people somewhere might think they are thereby trying to please God. You once asked yourself which was your greatest temptation, to be compulsive about appeasing a God who would otherwise snuff out your existence, or to stir yourself up to do anything at all about the calls of God, and you decided that during your lifetime, response needed your major energies. And so today again you joined the great company of makers of bread and wine and money who through the centuries have helped provide for this meal and for the words of God associated with it. You were glad to see that the family that brought forth the bread and wine today were new members for whom this act took on special importance. The offerings are needed—by the people who make them. Though the Lord's Supper is complete in its motion "for you," a response from you seals it.

DURING THE OFFERING, you have a chance to think about the bread and wine while the ministers prepare for the eucharist. Through the ages people have debated these simple gifts. The early church gave no prescription beyond the word *bread* and the word *wine*. It is probably best to stay relaxed about that simplicity. If the original meal was a Passover feast recalling the flight of the children of Israel from Egypt, the bread would lack leaven. Because Passover occurred in the spring, the wine by definition and chemical inevitability would have been fermented. But God can work through leavened or unleavened bread, and the wine could have been red or white. The idea of breaking one loaf preserves the biblical impulse best, as does sharing from one cup:

> The cup of blessing that we bless, is it not a participation in the blood of Christ? The bread that we break, is it not a participation in the body of Christ? Because there is one bread, we who are many are one body, for we all partake of the one bread (1 Corinthians 10:16–17).

If people find it more convenient to use many little bits of bread and many little cups, some of the pictorial element disappears, but the gift is still there. The picture then takes some explaining, just as Christians who in baptizing do not immerse people then have to draw verbal pictures in order to place proper emphasis on how baptism is a "burial" with Christ. You yourself found it more vivid when your congregation returned to the biblical custom of breaking one loaf and sharing one cup, but you didn't regard those who use other forms as weaker brothers and sisters. In fact, the more you thought about this debate, the less you thought about the character of bread and wine as such.

Someone has said that for the material side of the Christian faith, all you need are "a loaf of bread, a bottle of wine, and a river." Some people become nervous when you remind them that in this respect Christianity is a very material faith. They look for something spiritual and angelic, untouched and untainted by anything visible and earthly. Some Christians have turned their back on God's creation so much that they like to think of their faith as never touching the ground. The Letter to the Hebrews had to warn against that attitude (2:16–17): "For it is clear that he did not come to help angels, but the descendants of Abraham. Therefore he had to become like his brothers and sisters in every respect." The very material bread and wine come from the world of Christ's brothers and sisters, with whom he is concerned.

The chief thing in the sacrament is not a mysticism about natural elements. The use of bread and wine is not designed to lead you to a Walden Pond or an Orange County ravine, where you might commune with nature and thus become most intimate with God. This is not a festival of bread and wine as such. But why should anyone be nervous about connecting these gifts of earth, these natural gifts which are "for you," with the gifts of the eternal, the more than natural gifts which are "for you" as well? You resolve after today never again to look at a field of grain or a slope of grapes the casual way you did before. God is working through them and through the people who work with them. What comes from those very fields and vines might end up on the Lord's Table. Even if it does not, it can work to the purposes of God in other ways. You also resolve never to look again the same old way at the bread and wine of your own table. Why take for granted elements which God can use to make Christ present among us? An old German Christmas carole included these lines:

Tell abroad his goodness proudly,
Who our race hath honored thus,
That He deigns to dwell with us. . . .

Similarly, after this day you can tell about God's goodness proudly. He honored the earth by making use of its produce to dwell with us. Angels can fit in the plot somewhere, as can untainted and unstained realms of being. But the Lord's Supper brings us a Christ *along with* elements that come from a natural order that allows for rust in grain and rancidity in wine. Christ and creation go together better than you thought.

    A PRAYER and an exchange called THE PREFACE follow the offering. By preserving this exchange through the years, the church helped you retain some tone of praise before the meal: "Let us give thanks to the Lord our God. It is right to give him thanks and praise." And the SANCTUS, or "Holy, Holy, Holy," helped. You could picture Isaiah in the temple, having a vision of God. That helped bring a sense of the presence of God to your church. You could also hear in the "Hosanna" the shouts of the people who greeted Jesus on Palm Sunday when he entered Jerusalem. That lifted the service above the dreary and the ordinary. God, the "thrice holy," is present here.

Now in the Great Thanksgiving you are able to sustain this note of presence, this spirit of awe and praise through the whole celebration. Some churches call this extended prayer "the eucharistic prayer." You recall how church leaders have only recently begun to recover the wider understanding of the biblical meal. There was once a time for only "the words of institution," that stark and bare running together of the New Testament sayings of

Jesus in the upper room. Some weeks the ministers may still read only those words. You get the feeling that, when they do, it is because everyone is in a hurry, though there may be other good reasons to read only them from time to time.

You remember how as a child, back before your feet touched the church floor and before you could sit a full hour and a quarter, your parents would bring you to church on "Communion Sunday." You would hear these words of institution but not quite understand what was going on. If you recall correctly, it seemed as if everyone became very sad at this point in the service. That emotion was not completely out of place, because the words themselves do say that Jesus spoke them "in the night in which he was betrayed." It was then and is now a serious business to follow Jesus on his journey to the cross, and you have never quite come to terms with some of the modern liturgies that set out to celebrate but instead produce chiefly giddiness. So you do not want to make fun of the grimness of the old-style Communion. But something was missing in the overall attitude.

During confirmation instruction, you started learning more about the meaning of the Lord's Supper. Most of the instruction concerned itself with the words of institution. You knew *something* happened when the minister spoke them, but what? You watched the sign of the cross being made over the bread as you heard, "This is my body," and over the cup during "This cup is the new covenant in my blood." *That* must have been the moment when *it* happened; but, still, what was *it*? You puzzled everything out in a negative way. Adults told you, in effect, that our people believed less than did the people on the Christian right and more than the people on the left. On our right were Roman Catholics who, you were told, held a purely magical concept. They said that at this moment the bread and wine changed into the body and blood of Jesus, even though they kept on looking like the same bread and wine. On our left were other Christians who said that at this moment nothing happened to the bread and wine. The Lord's Supper was simply a memorial feast done "in remembrance of Jesus." The bread and wine were merely symbols of that pious people used in order to focus their minds on God.

You may have gotten it all wrong while everyone else got it right—one can never be sure about a child's grasp of difficult subjects. Maybe the issues seemed difficult only to you. But for all your questioning, you did find the church making a heavy investment in the words of institution without offering much of a positive understanding of the Lord's Supper. Never could you be content to hold to a view that was halfway between everyone else's without having much to say about your own position. Those old teachers of "our people," let it be said, were not all wrong. Medieval Roman Catholics were inclined to almost magical views, and even after the Reformation period Catholics did set down hard-line notions about how the substance of bread and wine changed. It was true that many of their devotions treated these substances as if they had supernatural curative powers. Popular piety may still do so. But contemporary statements of Roman Catholic faith about the sacramental presence of Christ are vastly different from those earlier approaches, and it is unfair to misrepresent the living faith of Catholic Christians today. Your theologians regularly sit down with them nowadays to discuss this presence of Christ, and the different parties cannot find any real differences between them. Maybe it is no fun for Christian factions to stop fighting. Certainly it is difficult to understand the Lord's Supper now, if formerly you depended on having an enemy position nearby to serve as a boundary against which you could prop up your own definition. But growth in the unity of the church of Christ more than compensates for those emotional losses.

On the other side, the so-called left side of the argument, it is not at all clear that everyone even in those days believed that bread and wine were *mere* bread and wine and that Jesus was *not* present in the meal except in the pious minds of the worshipers. In the religious battles of the sixteenth century, both sides of the Protestant debate exaggerated the differences and misrepresented alternative views. This is not to say that there were not and are not differences. *Your* theologians have not been as confident about coming to early agreement with non-Catholic Christianity about the Lord's Supper. But if Reformed Christianity still speaks often of the bread and wine as *symbols* of the body and blood, clearly the concept of symbol is changing. You are less likely to hear the elements spoken of as *mere* symbols, and whenever the word *mere* disappears, there is motion toward a new understanding. In any case, it is harder than it was four centuries ago for you to define your Lord's Supper when the people you were taught to call the enemy on the left change position.

The Great Thanksgiving or eucharistic prayer is a way of helping congregations come to a more positive and more fully biblical understanding of what went on in the first Lord' Supper. To say that at the Lord's Supper you should hear the bare words of institution because the Bible reports only on them, and because this economy will make your mass closer to the mass of Christ, is false. Jesus did in fact say prayers and blessings at that meal—we are confident of that, as confident as we can be of anything else about early Christian faith and worship. At the time of the Reformation, church leaders cut back on much of what they might have thought Jesus had said and done because in their time the eucharistic prayer had come to be locked in to what was called the canon of the mass.

And that meant it was linked to some ideas that were almost magical and to other ideas that suggested Christians were bringing sacrifices to please God. The Reformers could tolerate neither idea, so they swept the chancel clean by throwing out the whole eucharistic prayer.

Not having to fight that battle, at least not in the same way, Christians today are free to recover the larger biblical set of meanings. To continue to deprive you and other worshipers of these meanings by reading only the words of institution is to preserve an unfair and more modern (sixteenth-century) approach in place of the more ancient, conservative, and biblical (first-century) one.

You listen closely today as the minister leads you in the eucharistic prayer. The praise of the Father for the great gift of Jesus and for this meal continues. You keep alive an awareness of all creation, that creation from which comes the bread and wine on which you depend and through which the presence of God is known today. In this prayer you recall the sense of story, remembering how bound up with faith is the narrative about Abraham, Israel, and the prophets. Your prayer comes to its climax when you thank God for sending the Son. All this is a Christian reenactment of the praises and blessings that Jesus spoke in the words of institution when he gave thanks over the bread he broke and the cup he shared. The Holy Spirit, who "calls, gathers, enlightens, and sanctifies the whole Christian church" is God in action. This Spirit makes the "thrice holy" present in the here and now. You do not think of this remembrance of Christ as the annual meeting of a burial society. Neither is this narrative only a historical record about people of old. The Great Thanksgiving surrounds the present-making power of God. After this you find no need to go out hunting for ways to meet the Lord or to have an experience of God by your private enterprise, mental tricks, or the climbing of mystical ladders. This prayer celebrates the way God is with you and the congregation. It takes some act of energy and imagination now to deny God, to turn your back on the presence.

In this context, you now hear the words of institution exactly as you did years before, with startling clarity. But now the pressure is off them. You no longer find yourself wondering what kind of change is occurring during a ministerial sign of the cross over bread and wine. This prayer adds a word of Paul that connects your celebration with the people who do not yet share the presence: "For as often as we eat of this bread and drink from this cup, we proclaim the Lord's death until he comes." The congregation then erupts with three shouts in three tenses: "Christ has died. Christ is risen. Christ will come again."

Because the idea of mere remembrance is too weak to sustain the presence of God, it is easy to forget the specific command of Jesus to share this act "for the remembrance of me." So the Great Thanksgiving picks up the ideas of remembering and brings it into focus. "With this bread and cup we remember the life our Lord offered for us." He has come with this bread and cup, and now we remember him with it. The former use is instrumental: Christ makes an agent of bread and wine. He uses it to come to your midst. God comes with it "for you . . . for forgiveness." You then naturally look ahead, as Jesus did, toward another kind of reunion with him. "Believing the witness of his resurrection," you reborn people "await his coming in power to share with us the great and promised feast."

You respond with early Christians: "Amen. Come, Lord Jesus." One side of your mind does not want the end of human history to come so soon. You want to see your children grow to maturity. You have a friendly meal with neighbors planned for late afternoon. You love this world since you have come to know its natural wonders.

But "Come, Lord Jesus" reminds you that the Lord of history has more in store for you than stretched-out rainy Sunday afternoons, the treadmill, the rat race, one thing after another, and an otherwise purposeless existence.

The Great Thanksgiving closes with a call for the Holy Spirit to be present. Today you hear much about the presence of the Holy Spirit. A charismatic or pentecostal movement in the churches, including your church, is making special efforts to realize and claim this presence. You personally may have not been attracted to the movement, though you welcome some of the vitalities it brings wherever it does not divide congregations and make second-class Christians of those who do not join it. But the charismatics are not in the forefront of your mind at this hour. You are about the way the Holy Spirit is called for and comes with this gathering, with this bread and wine of a sacred meal. Who could ask anything more than this kind of awesome intimacy? "Send now, we pray, your Holy Spirit, the spirit of our Lord and of his resurrection, that we who receive the Lord's body and blood may live to the praise of your glory and receive our inheritance with all your saints in light." This meal is to become effective in your life, and for that the Holy Spirit must be the agent. "Amen. Come, Holy Spirit." With the answer to this prayer in the form of the coming of the Holy Spirit, you have to be ready for a changed life. Your body, the one that will soon receive the gift of God in the eating of this meal, is also a temple of the Holy Spirit. Take care of it. Take care.

You do not have much time to think during the last few lines of the Great Thanksgiving, but you try today, as you have tried before, to let your imagination soar as you hear: "Join our prayers with those of your servants of every time and every place. . . ." The grand prayer of blessing over the bread and the cup is also a way of affirming the whole church. Those servants of every time and place include a vast and diverse company but also some very specific persons known well to you. Not only the huddled Eastern Europeans, the charismatic Christians of Chile, the disciples in the upper room, the smugglers of bread and wine into concentration camps, but also those new parents just two pews ahead, the people being baptized today who will share this table for the first time, and . . . you. You the sinner. You the servant. You, you the saint. Sensing the breadth and the depth, you find it easy to utter a doxology, a song of praise to the Holy Trinity: "Through him, with him, in him, in the unity of the Holy Spirit, all honor and glory is yours, Almighty Father, now and forever."

During the doxology, the minister ordinarily lifts the bread and the cup, even holds them high. Call Martin Luther in to explain why:

> It signifies that Christ has commanded us to remember him. For just as the sacrament is bodily elevated, and yet Christ's body and blood are not seen in it, so he is also remembered and elevated by the word of the sermon and is confessed and adored in the reception of the sacrament. In each case he is apprehended only by faith; for we cannot see how Christ gives his body and blood for us and even now daily shows and offers it before God to obtain grace for us.

You have never heard those words before, but they do set off a chain of reflection about the presence of Christ. you postpone such reflection until the time for Communion, when you do not want to have an idle mind.

Suddenly, you are praying your table prayer for the meal. it is not "God is great, God is good," "Come, Lord Jesus," "The eyes of all wait upon thee," or any of the other table graces you use at home. instead you join in praying The LORD'S PRAYER, the "Our Father" that Christ taught his people. The meal follows.

Just as Jesus, being a Jew at a special dinner, would have taken some bread and wine before he passed or carried it to others, so the minister takes some or receives it from one of the Communion assistants, and then the congregation participates. Your turn comes and you hear, "The body of Christ, given for you. . . . the blood of Christ shed for you." "For you": The plural is singular now. It is into your hand that the minister places the bread, and it is your mouth that receives the cup. You do not stop being a member of the congregation—no act besides this brings you closer to others—but just as you must die for yourself, you must also believe for yourself and receive for yourself. You may sense the presence of God when you recall your baptism, or at prayer, or in hearing the word of God. But few moments in life reach you as directly as does this weekly opportunity at the Lord's Supper.

What are you thinking as you receive the bread and wine, or when you return to your chair and listen to the choir and the organ, or, sometimes better, when you enjoy the silence broken only by the footfall of the communing people and the word "for you" spoken to each? What are you thinking as you join in the brief hymn to the LAMB OF GOD who "takes away the sin of the world"?

The act of communing takes but seconds, and participating in a congregational COMMUNION takes only a few minutes. Today, as so often before, you resolved to use the time to good advantage. Will you have done so? Admit it, some days your resolve goes as quickly as it came. You were going to concentrate on the "for you . . . for forgiveness." Instead your mind wandered, and you cannot later recall anything at all of what passed through it. Not a trace of ecstasy went with this personal moment in the meal. You were in the presence of God and, had it not been for the slight nervousness you felt going up to the front of an assembly, you might have stifled a yawn. You let some passing thing distract you. A scuff on the shoe of the minister. The choir singing a bit flat. A candle dripping on the new church carpet. Had you remembered to have the spot removed from the back of your coat? Who donated those altar flowers? Will I get a raise this week?

Here you are, back in your seat. Should you feel guilty about having let the moment pass? Isn't it just human nature to have a wandering mind? You really don't believe the people who claim they can clear their heads and have pure and constant contact with God. There must be a lot of hypocrites here. Why did so little happen?

4. Reflections during Communion

THE MINUTES OF REFLECTION DURING COMMUNION do not allow time for developing a well-rounded theology. Indeed, they hardly suffice for sustaining a simple sequence of serious thought. But one can use this time, with or without some hymns or prayers, to place a few little mental levers on a few spiritual fulcrums, in order to lift them at other times, in other places. One might reflect, for example, on the feelings experienced, the forgiveness received, the presence promised, or the commitment entailed.

Experience

What am I supposed to feel? Am I *supposed* to feel? The whole idea of receiving forgiveness of sins implies recognizing how far you are from God and in how much need you stand. But what if you do not *feel* guilty or agonized?

You have to admit that different personality types will react differently. William James described "the sick soul" and "healthy-minded" as psychological models. The sick soul will have no difficulty feeling in need of forgiveness. The trembling of a leaf has made hearts leap in fear from Leviticus to Martin Luther to modern times. The whole universe seems then to be personified. It takes the form of the accusing finger of God. The victim of such sin-sickness may simply be working out some problem left over from a bad childhood. Parents placed too many restrictions on the conscience, and adult life became nothing more than a "Do I dare?" or "Someone is watching!" Such a person hesitates to take bold action, fearing the consequences.

When time for confession comes, such a sick soul is likely a junkie let loose in a pharmacy: All the options are there, in dazzling array. If you are a sin-sick soul, as the psalmist was when he made a river of his bed because of tears, you are able to spill out whole catalogs of faults. So you examine the recesses of the hear and there find every kind of ugliness. You have not done anything worse than anyone else, but you feel worse. You know that before God the greatest faults, while they may mess up human relations more than do the sneaky little faults, violate above all the divine image. True, God forgives them as completely as others, but you still feel they demand a heroic assault.

Once upon a time you were taught to load up everything for a twice-monthly crusade against sins at Communion. If you were fortunate, your church encouraged private confession. While you could and should always confess your faults to the person you offended, all faults, especially hidden ones, were faults against God. The minister became a representative person who could speak as it were for God. Ministerial words also became symbolic ways of hearing the human race reaffirm you. They personified the congregation. God was gracious, but now the human family was shown to include "gracious others."

If you did not make a private confession, every Communion service included a group opportunity for exposing your sinfulness to God through rite and ceremony. If such confessions stood the risk of turning routine—and you had to admit that the pose of the average congregation suggested that most people were pretty casual about what they were saying and doing—for you, at times at least, they were wonderful instruments for unburdening. You placed your sin on the strong shoulders of Christ, and the minister in the name of God absolved you of, or forgave, those sins. Somehow you had to work out a logic by which you again brought them to the Lord's Table only minutes later. Since *it* was "for forgiveness," you were to leave sins there and walk back to the pew refreshed, with a clean slate on which to start piling up a whole new batch of sins.

Seriously, you knew that this script was not how it was supposed to work. Popular piety had things a bit wrong here. When you gathered your thoughts in an adult study class, the accent was different. There you heard a translation of the phrase *simul iustus et peccator*: You are at the same time the just person made just by the act of Christ, and the sinner kept sinful by your humanity and your acts. "At the same time" meant that when God looked at you in Christ, through Christ, because of Christ—which figuratively meant at you in your baptismal robes, identified with Christ, or here at supper with him—God did not see you as a half-safe, half-sinful being. You were not 99 and $^{44}/_{100}$ percent clean and every day in every way getting better and better through positive thinking about the cross. No, God looked at you and saw Christ. Insofar as God made you just through the grace of Christ, which you received in faith, you lacked nothing.

"At the same time" also meant that the God who looked at you when you stood apart from Christ saw nothing to like. This God was not impressed by your claim to have met the Lord. A bumper sticker asserting that you were born again or had received the Holy Spirit meant no more spiritually than do the annual rival claims that a certain state is number one in football. In fact, your greatest temptation—not to need God—occurred precisely in your spiritual life. When competitive Christian television programs teach you how to praise God better than others, and to be more pious than others, there is a danger that you will use your praise and piety to bind God, to take away the freedom of God. You will be saying, "Notice me, Lord!" All the while you are therefore not relying in faith on the gift of Jesus Christ. You are busy parading virtues, and God is saying, "Forget it! Your virtues at their best are not good enough."

The fact that you feel the need to do such parading suggests that you are a sick soul and need a remedy. You have come, then, to the right place. There is no magical transaction called confession/absolution, or confession/Lord's Supper. But in the meal you receive the gifts of Jesus Christ. You did not earn them and you did not earn a place at this banquet, but by baptism you are identified and united with Christ. As in baptism you symbolically came out from under the water, gasping for life because you had been "dead." (In the Christian scheme, you did already die and rise with Christ.) When you go to the Lord's Supper, then, as you kneel you are not bringing your adding-machine totals of the sins you want forgiven. You are bringing your whole self in need, and with the loaf and the cup you are receiving the forgiveness that assures you that your whole self is full of well-being.

You know, then, what you are supposed to feel.

William James also spoke of the religion of "the healthy-minded." He thought it was especially attractive to those who joined the Christian Science movement, liberal Protestantism, or something that was then called New Thought. Such people believed that there was an essential harmony to the universe, that all they had to do was tap into it. Mortal mind or negative thinking might interrupt the flow, but a person could realize a return to the original harmony. Such systems are at odds with Christianity, which claims a disruption of the harmony. Humans create discord and chaos. They do not hear the purity of the angels on the morning of creation. They do not stir to the trumpets of the messengers of God. They toot their own horns and sing their own praises. Well-being is not part of the flow. It is a divine gift that interrupts all our natural ways of expecting wholeness.

While healthy-mindedness as a system is beyond the scope of the Lord's Supper, the healthy-minded psychological style is present among Christians. The Bible and Christian history display characters who did not make a river of their beds with tears. Martin Luther may have felt threatened by a thousand devils and by a judging God who was too near, but in your healthy-mindedness you do not. You see no point in pretending. You find nothing especially attractive or Christian in those otherwise blithe people who think they please God by bowing lowest, kneeling longest, and groveling most visibly: "Look, God, I really got good at confessing."

The healthy-minded or blithe Christian type is a personality that, fully aware of the fallenness of creation, grasps its beauty inside. After the resurrection of Christ, the first signs of a new order, a new creation, are here for affirming. This kind of Christian takes bits of sand and dye, fuses them, and produces stained glass through which you see the sun break on the sanctuary floor with a foretaste of heavenly sparkles. The New Creation Christian takes the disordered sounds of diesel engines, clanging pots, and scuffling feet and reorders them into scales and tones until you hear overtones of the music of spheres. This Christian walks the hospital corridors aware of death but sings quiet songs because God is also at work healing. Healthy-mindedness is not positive thinking apart from God but a psychological and spiritual bearing that finds God to be not the Judge but the One who intended and intends concord.

The blithe type lives with spiritual hazards that are as great as those brought by the grovelers. If you find yourself in the healthy-minded part of the spectrum, you may use the Lord's Supper as a time to become especially alert to these dangers. The silences for self-examination are excellent opportunities for this. You might be riding for a fall. That is, you may be sunny about your faith because you have not yet been tested. No cloud has yet shadowed you. Wait until you find that your child is suffering from a debilitating disease. Let an economic disaster wipe out your assets. Some day someone important to you will find great fault with you and announce a breach. For all the smiles in the world, you cannot backslap your way into a new relation. Then some of the illusions with which you lived will drop.

Healthy-mindedness may employ a faulty spiritual diagnosis. You have heard the familiar statements of what Dietrich Bonhoeffer calls cheap grace: "I like to commit sins. God likes to forgive them. The world is admirably arranged." Or, "I can sin; that's my business. God will forgive; that's the business God is in. We will keep each other busy." These are flippant translations of attitudes that color many easy lives. None of them measures the cost to God of the cross or the cost to humans of discipleship. Unless a grain of wheat falls into the ground and dies, it becomes nothing. But if it dies, it brings forth fruit. No one follows Jesus without taking up a cross and denying the self. Jesus knew what was in humans and searchingly stripped the disciples themselves of their claims upon God—because Jesus loved his disciples and did not want them to rule God out of their lives by their casualness.

In order to be sure that healthy-minded psychological types come to spiritual depth, the preacher in every sermon will proclaim the law of God. In some contexts, the law of God is God's power that enables one to see what it is that care of the neighbor establishes. But in the present context, the law of God does nothing but accuse. You thought you were doing right because you did not kill? Jesus says that if you hate, you are a murderer. You thought you were pretty healthy because you stayed married and faithful to one partner and never committed

adultery? You all have committed adultery when you
merely looked, or even thought, lustfully. Martin Luther
liked to say that if you did not feel sinful you should
reach inside your clothes and pinch yourself to see if you
are still flesh and blood.

What are you supposed to feel? In some epochs and
some congregations, preachers and counselors have to
cool people off. Don't feel so much, they say; you are so
busy enjoying your miseries that you do not even recognize that there is a Physician who has cured. But you, if
you are healthy-minded, live in a different kind of age and
place. Most sermons urge you to probe yourself more
deeply. But you can build a wall against God if you start
making the relation with God the basis of your own self-
esteem; that will not work. The preacher's admonition to
self-examination need not force you to change your personality type or your outlook on the new Creation. It only
asks you to be serious. You are to see things not through
illusion but as they are. The Christian faith calls you to
realism about the disharmonious universe in which babies
die, the innocent die, and you will die. There is a funda-
mental lack of fit in the way the world is now put together
apart from Christ, and its misfit character will not go
away this side of eternity, despite the victory of Christ.

What, then, are you supposed to feel? If not sniveling,
woebegone, sub-Christian blues, you are to acquire
awareness. You who are called "miserable sinners" may
not feel miserable. But like occupants of an aircraft in
which a time bomb is set in the baggage compartment,
though you feel fine about your martini and your magazine, you are in need of rescue. You need help. At the
Lord's Table it is not necessary for you to conjure up all
kinds of *emotions*; you simply need to be *aware* of need
and to realize the forgiveness of sins.

Forgiveness

Some weeks at the Lord's Supper you might wish to set your lever for reflection under another great burden: the concept of forgiveness. That this forgiveness of sins is "for you" is now clear by everything in the event, but what *is* forgiveness? Do we exaggerate its importance?

Jesus made much of it when he chose to forgive a person in need of physical healing, even though that meant offending the religious leaders. Give those leaders credit. They asked, with a proper sense of regard for holy things, "Who can forgive sins but God?" They were not likely to cheapen forgiveness. Paul busied himself with writing letters telling people how the forgiven should learn to live together as Jew and Gentile, male and female, enslaved and free. But along the way he spent much energy detailing what forgiveness meant for him and his readers. Throughout Christian history, Augustine, Bernard of Clairvaux, Martin Luther, John Calvin, and a large company of others described forgiveness as a central image for the basic movement of a loving God to mortals.

So it is that today we have inherited something we can call "the doctrine of the forgiveness of sins." Whole church bodies claim it as their possession. It is their badge and banner. With it they make their claim, "We're number one!" They use it to show what all the second-bests look like, because the others own lesser chunks of the doctrine or because they have it all wrong. In the nineteenth century, Americans paraded the Monroe Doctrine opposing European influence in the Western Hemisphere. One night a man was tarred and feathered and run out of town. A stranger came upon the victim and asked him what had happened. It seems that there had been a loyalty test and a dispute about this aspect of foreign policy. What had the tarred man said or done wrong? He answered, "I didn't say I don't love the Monroe Doctrine. I do love the Monroe Doctrine. I live by the Monroe Doctrine. I would die for the Monroe Doctrine. I simply said I don't know what it is." We wonder whether the people with the tar pots and baskets of feathers knew.

You are at the Lord's Table, assured that the forgiveness of sins comes "for you." It is easy to think, "I belong to the right club. I can show God the right credentials. I am loyal to my tribe. I love the doctrine of the forgiveness of sins. I would die for the doctrine of the forgiveness of sins. But I simply do not know what it is." If so, you have difficulty reflecting on Holy Communion. You wish to do better.

First of all, remember that a doctrine does not save. God saves. You need not even call it a doctrine, especially in times when many people use that word to suggest that the life has already gone out of a reality. In their minds— and why play into their problems?—a doctrine is a gravestone you place over the bones of something that once lived. It is a boundary you place around something your ancestors found important. A doctrine or a dogma is an attempt by humans to define the indefinable, to step across the boundaries of mystery and speak overconfidently about the secrets of God. In a time when people do not know who they are, they use the idea of a doctrine to set boundaries. In that case, a doctrine is not a witness to their love of truth but a mark of their sense of mutual suspicion. Since you cannot trust anyone, you have to ask whether they line up on the wrong or right side of a precisely defined doctrine. The fact that doctrines and dogmas have other, better uses is not of much help here. Let other people on other days rescue the concept of doctrine. You are a hungry person needing food, not recipe books. You seek the forgiveness of sins at the Lord's Supper.

Second, because in church you have time for clarity but not research, you might want some day to study the way the forgiveness of sins may be an obsolete badge of distinction for a church body or two. The Spirit of God works surprises these days, and the spread of divine grace is sufficiently broad that what once looked like a unique property or witness of an evangelical church now turns up on many hands. More than four centuries ago, reformers of the church looked around and honestly did see some Christians turning God's gift of forgiveness into a human transaction. People were using their energies to impress God. The faithful bought or visited relics, went on pilgrimages, pursued processions, paid for masses, purchased indulgences, and did what they could to buy the favorable attention of God. They were just as often busy piling up merits to impress God, so that God dared not act unfavorably to people who were owed so much for having helped keep the universe on track. No matter how ecumenical one's spirit, those pages of history cannot be obscured. Roman Catholics, heirs of that unreformed Christianity, today point this out in very public scholarship.

Unreformed Christianity underwent reform. You will hear some people who feel called to draw boundaries for God saying that wrong teachings about forgiveness are still on those other churches' books. Maybe it would be nice if church bodies did feel obliged to retrace their steps to all the old libraries and councils, call new councils, and bring out their erasers. But churches do not work that way. They write with far more vivid new inks over fading pages. Today it is more valuable to listen to evangelical Catholic sermons, where the message of the forgiveness of sins comes through loud and clear. *The Jerusalem Bible*, which Catholic scholars and publishers would like to see in every home, is a highly public document. Its footnoted versions stress the free gift of the forgiveness of sins in every crucial passage. This is disappointing to some left-over anti-Catholics. What fun is the Lord's Supper if there are fewer people to be *anti-* as we enjoy it? But a Christian spirit also impels you to express joy for the spread of grace. This realization, plus common agreement over the meaning of Christ's presence in the Lord's Supper, has built a sense of holy but not yet constant frustration among many Roman and other Catholic Christians. Why do we stay apart at the Lord's Table? Who are we to build fences where the Host does not?

Third, you do not need the words forgiveness *of sins* to express the new relationship you have to God in Christ. In some ways, these words can be code words, a metaphor through which Christians can connect with many biblical themes. Through most of the pages of the Hebrew scriptures (the Old Testament), repentance and forgiveness are not the prime statements. Yet the Old Testament is the church's book. God was active among his people. This God was a loving, caring, and yes, forgiving agent. The Hebrew scriptures busied themselves with talking about how God was shaping a people and covenanting with them out of steadfast love.

In the Gospels, Jesus is the bearer of forgiveness, but forgiveness is not the only word on his lips. Jesus calls for obedience. He asks for discipleship. Because, for many people, forgiveness symbolizes the basic trajectory of God's movement to humans, they expect to hear about nothing else. Yet Jesus does what the situation demands. When someone is ill, Jesus *may* be abrupt: "Your sins are forgiven!" But just as often he may simply heal the physical illness, and we do not hear about outcomes having to do with forgiveness. His Good Samaritan is someone who pours on oil and wine and foots the bill for the clinic, without—so far as we know—passing out tracts or preaching sermons on forgiveness.

Paul, who had persecuted the church, found it easy to feel agony over guilt. He was tortured by his need for forgiveness. So he became a proclaimer par excellence of that teaching. But, as we already noted, he spent as much time telling the forgiven how to live together, or to have holy lives, as to be forgiven. So you, too, do not need to have a specific code word or formula in mind when you want to realize the gift of the Lord's Supper.

When your church wrote its older books of worship and teaching, debate over forgiveness was prime. Martin Luther was of the sick-souled type, who projected his struggles from the monastery onto the movement that followed him. In the modern play *Luther*, John Osborne has Luther railing against the empty heavens, as if God were remote: "God is dead." The real Luther had the opposite problem. For him the heavens were full and close, and God was too near, too threatening. A holy God might annihilate an unholy human. Divine perfection could not coexist with human imperfections. The monk tried every rule and every discipline, but still each trembling leaf caused him to cower. When, in the writings of Paul, Luther discovered the forgiveness of sins, the monk naturally chose to use it as the basic image of the loving divine movement.

Today, it is often noted, many people have a different problem. They are there with John Osborne's fictional Luther. Their God is remote. Where Luther asked, "Is God gracious?" they ask, "Is God?" Their doubts may not lead them to verge on simple atheism. Such Christians put their problem in different ways. They will complain about the lack of meaning in their lives. Where once the simplest peasants could endure every kind of setback because God would reward them in heaven, now eternal life has become a very vague concept for them. While once God seemed to be pronouncing a perpetual benediction on their towns, so that all knew their places, now urban life seems plotless. Typical words that people use—perhaps you used—to describe the modern condition in which most of us share are alienation, brokenness, and meaninglessness. We seek reconciliation, wholeness, and meaning.

Say words like *reconciliation, wholeness,* and *meaning,* and you come very close to the center of Christian witness. Jesus Christ reconciles God to humans, and humans to each other. Wholeness virtually serves as a synonym for salvation, for well-being under God. Jesus Christ the risen one brings meaning because he is the first sign of the New Creation, the new order of being. It is hard to see why anyone should feel guilty about using words like these to express the experience of grace in the Lord's Supper. Christ the physician offers the gift of a cure for what ails us. If he and we have varying names for the disease—and thus, in a way, subtly, different diseases—we shall welcome marvelously varied remedies. Forgiveness of sins, then, is a blanket term for the whole relationship that Jesus affects and which is "for you" in the Lord's Supper when grasped by faith.

While writing these pages, I had occasion to consult Edmund Schlink's *Theology of the Lutheran Confessions* to see what he and they had to say on this subject. Under the category "Forgiveness," the index said, "see Gospel; Justification: Lord's Supper; Word of God." Under three of those four categories, "Forgiveness" did not appear at all; the book treats it as a synonym for *gospel* and *justification*! Under "Word of God," there are seven brief references to the subcategory "of forgiveness." One of these citations does suggest synonymity: "forgiveness of sins is the same as justification" in the confessional writings. And Schlink develops a thesis: "The Gospel is the word of forgiveness of sins and justification because of Christ."

When we introduce the *–ation* words, like *justification*, it is easy to clutter and confuse the mind of a modern person who wants to experience forgiveness, to realize wholeness, in the event of the Lord's Supper. How are you to think of what the code words suggest? Most important is the idea that you do not bring something with which to impress God. God shatters whatever is in your hand. The law of God accuses and annihilates you. Then God, acting through and because of Christ, creates a new you, a baptized person-in-Christ. That is what it means to be a forgiven person, to experience an act or a motion of divine forgiveness.

You can now see why this forgiveness is the core of Holy Communion. The body and blood of Christ in the Lord's Supper are the body and blood of Christ on the cross. The cross was for you, and so is the Supper. In the meal, the cross is a present-day reality. The risen and ascended Christ is present in this form and at this event. Just as preaching, received in faith, is not mere talk about forgiveness but actually works forgiveness, so the Lord's Supper, received in faith, is not a pageant displaying the story of a forgiving God. It is God in action, affecting forgiveness, creating the new. The *Large Catechism* uses vivid language about the Lord's Supper not as a prescription but as a remedy:

> For here in the sacrament you receive from Christ's lips the forgiveness of sins, which contains and conveys God's grace and Spirit with all his gifts, protection, defense, and power against death and the devil and all evils.

Maybe you had not quite counted on having to take on "the devil and all evils," but this remedy is designed to help you do just that. And there may be a better way of conceiving what is wrong than the way of superficial diagnoses about personality types, symptoms of imbalance, Oedipal complexes, or maladjustment to the modern condition. The Lord's Supper is "the food of the soul since it nourishes and strengthens the new person." It is "a pure, wholesome, soothing medicine which aids and quickens in both soul and body. For where the soul is healed, the body has benefited also." Here is another bonus, and you do not have to join a therapeutic club in the church to share the benefit.

Forgiveness means liberation. Classically, this liberation refers to freedom from sin, death, and the devil. But it is possible to hear of this only in the context of middle-class America and not to envision all the other settings in which Christians look for liberation. In the concentration camps the Lord's Supper meant forgiveness of sins, but it also depicted a zone of human freedom into which believers hoped God would lead them again. Under governments that repress the faith, communicants cannot help but include their prayers and hopes for escape from such bondage. Today in Latin America and elsewhere in the Third World, Christians hungry for political and economic freedom have developed a "liberation theology." In its terms, worshipers want the Lord's Supper to be freed from the cozy bindings in which the rich celebrate it.

To the liberation theologian, many biblical motifs have come to be neglected by churches in prosperous nations. Throughout the Old Testament, the Lord of Israel is especially active among the poor and overrun. Jesus Christ clearly announces that he has also come to the oppressed and wants to work for change in their lives. In that thrust, the death of Jesus and the Lord's Supper are gifts to the poor and oppressed, who, it is said, feel less the weight of sin than they do the bondage produced by the people who exploit them. Such reasoning is understandable among people who know little freedom and have nothing earthly to look forward to under their present regimes. Secure and well-off Christians do well not to judge these brothers and sisters but to understand them when they tie together their dreams of political freedom on the one hand with their grasp of grace and liberation from sin on the other. The two are not the same thing, but freedom is contagious, and acts of imagination can help Christians everywhere share on another's aspirations and hopes that God will act.

Obsession with the term *forgiveness of sins* has sometimes led partisans to narrow the meanings of the Lord's Table. They feel it wrong to connect eucharist or thanksgiving with the Supper because it may detract from the main theme. Yet the Great Thanksgiving is wholly preoccupied with being thankful to the loving God who not only created the world but who also establishes in it a new relation with you. Others see forgiveness as in competition with the idea of Communion, which some churches make central. But this is also unnecessarily cramping. Another of the Lutheran confessions connects the two: The same Lord's Supper that forgives is also "a true bond and union of Christians with Christ their head and with one another." We are, through this gift, "incorporated into the body of Christ, which is the church." Because we and others share unmerited forgiveness, we are on the same level at the Lord's Table. We have to be very careful about placing different levels where God does not, and about ruling people away whom Christ includes at his Supper.

Presence

What do we mean by the presence of Christ in this Supper? Perhaps if one could compute all the serious reflections that people bring to the Table, this issue of the presence would rank third. Whoever studies the history of dispute over the sacrament or listens to present-day theological debate might conclude that it is the number one issue. Why? It provides grist for intellectual debate and becomes a kind of test for people who like to sharpen their philosophical tools on things sacred. Being a historian of Christianity, I find it hard to look at the record without adding that if there is any feature of the Lord's Supper that brings out the meanest growls from partisan Christians, this is it. While the faithful people have the least difficulty with them, and while the New Testament offers almost no light, the subject naturally comes up in the mind of anyone who wants to be neat and inclusive in thought about the Lord's Supper.

To begin at the end, most writers on the subject say that the precise mode of Christ's presence is a mystery. Then they define mystery not as you do in a mystery story, where by the end of the book everything is clear— the butler did it, there is a conclusion, and the mystery ends. In a deeper sense, mystery means rather that if you pull away one veil, another will still cover the subject; one could pull back veils for all the years that history gives and still not have exposed the subject to clear view. Emphatically, the presence of Christ is such a mystery. There can be honest and creative addresses to mystery, such as people make when they witness to the character of God, and less valid ones, of the sort one reads when people convince themselves they really have proved the existence of God or have philosophically explained away the origin and presence of evil.

The special problem with the presence of Christ in the Lord's Supper grows from the fact that the Scriptures are so nearly silent about it. This means that the Lord's Supper is used to fill in the blanks. Other teachings are like barnacles attached to it, and it gets connected to other doctrines. Of course, it links with one's concept of where the risen and exalted Jesus Christ is, and whether Christ can reveal the fullness of God in earthly and finite forms. We leave those filled-in blanks and connected doctrines for other authors in other books for other days. You have the Lord's Supper on your mind.

Bring up the presence of Christ and you enter the zone where intellectuality has made its greatest mark on practice. In some churches, one gets the impression that to escape unworthiness—Paul's term for the unexamined life at the Lord's Supper—one must have a certain IQ. It would seem to be necessary for communicants to be able to mouth a precise number of memorized catechismal formulas. The church might make exception for the people in homes for the mentally disabled, who are allowed to get by on simple affirmations of faith in Jesus Christ and a desire for the Lord's Table. But beyond them, those who merit access to Communion are those who have the prescriptions down cold. The present-day church is trying to learn how to hold together two ideas: the integrity of understanding the Lord's Supper and the need not to impose barriers that the Pauline and Gospel accounts clearly do not impose. At the very least, one can learn not to attribute a mean spirit and bad faith to other Christians who are at least as concerned as you are to be faithful to the documents and the truth but who come off with a different reading.

You will never find an intellectually satisfying formula for the presence. Write that down and remember it as you read all the books, by people on your side and by others. In the end, the honest writers all have to lapse back for a second to the language about mystery, where they began. Some of them succeed at representing accurately their own church's teaching; they deserve awards from historical societies. Others ingeniously connect their personal philosophy to the teaching; they merit rewards from philosophical societies, though it is hard to picture a single philosopher likely to be impressed. My tone here might verge on the satirical and the anti-intellectual. I do not intend that, since I too respect and ever regard as necessary the idea of "loving God with all the mind" and extending this to the mode of Christ's presence in the Lord's Supper. But here is a case in which it is necessary to expect only small returns on expensive investments.

The Lord's Supper service has room for some ethereal images like that of the "thrice-holy" that faced Isaiah in the temple. But at the most personal point the sacrament is very physical. Just as God is revealed in the bad grammar of the well-preached word, so now you have to think in rather crass terms about another mode of the presence. The same kind of bread you will eat at home this noon is on the table. The wine here is similar to what you can have at dinner. You pass them through the same mouth. They carry the same germs. One may harden, the other turns sour, like any other bread and wine. People with bad breath and cavities receive them past droopy mustaches or elegantly tinted lips. Keep the crude images in mind, since no other ones will keep to the forefront the offense and the scandal. The food will pass through the body and be digested and excreted through natural processes. Jesus knew all about that when he pointed to bread and said, "This—my body!" and when he lifted a cup and gave it with "This—my blood!" (Some scholars think that, where the Greek text uses the much fought-over word is, the language Jesus spoke led him simply to designate.)

You move to the Table and are given the gifts with the words "The body of Christ. . . . The blood of Christ," not the "bread of the earth, the wine of the vine." What are you to think? Christ is somehow present in form as body, not as ghost. Christ is present in the whole church and in this congregation, in the whole event of the Lord's Supper—but also here and now. Christ is not naturally at home in your heart; there is no room for him there. But now more-than-naturally he finds room through your whole body, through faith, which also means because you hear the word promising his coming, and you cling to that promise. The promise means God recognized that in faith you accept the gift of Christ's presence, and God sees you as "one body" with all others who are in Christ, who receive this body and blood. When the minister hands over the bread or the cup, this handing over takes the same trajectory as the whole shape of God's act in Christ: Christ is handed over to evil people and for the sake of life.

One contemporary pondering, Robert Jenson's *Visible Words*, points to certain problems connected with two main theories about the presence. The first depends on the power of consecration—remember that ministerial sign of the cross above the bread and wine and how you thought *now* they are being changed? This approach set out to show how God, who can do anything, could make two things into one without destroying either. This is not an unintelligent approach, but it is an unnecessary one. The people who made so much of the act of consecrating were not too interested in explaining the presence. They wanted, as you do not, to carve out a role for the priesthood, to give priests a monopoly on something. Nothing worked better for this than to assert the exclusive right of the priest to a consecrating act that made two things one and yet kept them two things. Today Roman Catholicism has moved far from this concept, though it is still busy redefining evangelical priesthood.

Another way to explain the presence is to use spiritual language in order to remove distance. Yes, it says, by faith we can see that Jesus overleaps distance and is "at the right hand of the Father." Since distances mean nothing in the spiritual realm, that right-hand position extends here to the altar where the bread and wine are.

But this approach makes Christ's presence conditional on your ability to imagine him being far and near; the presence is not straightforward here. This understanding also seems to shrink from the idea that the divine or the human can ever be embodied. Christians cannot leap out of their bodies to be spiritually with Christ at the right hand of the Father.

A third approach is more radical than these. The body of the risen Christ is not separated from any reality. Christ has risen in the body to be where God is. God is everywhere. If the risen Christ is, according to promise, embodied where the bread and this cup are, the only miracle you need to believe in is Christ's own resurrection. God is present wherever the promises of God are in effect. These promised are embodied. God has a body where these promises connect to the man Christ Jesus, or to this event called the Lord's Supper and the bread and the cup that are at its heart.

This bread and wine are, in the eyes of God, the presence of the man Jesus. No other body and blood of Christ are to be found by means of better telescopes in farther ranges of distance above the clouds. The risen Jesus is risen to new spiritual and bodily life, so we can now be audacious about the promises and say that the bread and the cup *are* the body. But this is true only for faith. The presence is hidden. The bread does not look like his body, and it did not do so when first he made the designation and offered the promise about his embodiment in the meal. There is more to Christ than this local and temporal presence. This "more" has to do with Christ's future when the word will be preached and when the bread and wine will be enjoyed again in this event. That is why after the service today the ministers—or anyone—can consume the leftover wine and bread. Forget about the elements then. If their power as Christ's body depended upon consecration, you would have to deconsecrate them or save them for ongoing power. The choice you make shows how you regard this event.

Within our lifetime, it is not likely that all Christians will come to agree on this or on any other version of the presence. Remember my first words in this connection: These efforts could do no more than draw away some veils while leaving others to surround the mystery.

Commitment

You may find it valuable to reflect on still one other feature of the Lord's Supper. What does this event have to do with our way of life?

By concentrating on what passes through our minds during the liturgy, we have sounded rather churchy and even churchy. These reflections might have the smell of incense and the glow of candles about them, and thus they lose contact with the surrounding world. Yet you may spend all but a couple of your 168 weekly hours outside the sanctuary. Debates about catechism and dogma will almost never come up there. The test of this Lord's Supper and its workings will be in the lives of communicants.

In the oldest words we have about this meal, in First Corinthians, Paul concerned himself with connecting Communion practices with the lives of the participants. Many of them lived in open scandal. That had to stop. Others made a noisy orgy out of the eucharist itself. Paul drew the congregation up short with questions: "The cup of blessing which we bless, is it not a participation in the blood of Christ? The bread which we break, is it not a participation in the body of Christ?" (1 Corinthians 10:16-17). That word *participation* is an urgent link between the liturgy and Jesus Christ and then between Jesus Christ and all the rest of life. An exchange is going on here; in fact, behind the Greek word translated *participation* stands the word *exchange*. In a sense, Jesus Christ, the Son of God and divine Savior, exchanges roles when he takes on flesh, humbles himself, gives himself in this bread and wine, and suffers death. And for that reason you undergo an exchange and get to share in the divine gifts and life.

No one should walk away from the Lord's Supper unchanged. It is good to use the visibility of Communion and its bodily actions as an occasional means to reflect on personal commitment. You may have heard some experts advise that congregations be kept busy singing hymns during Communion so that they will not accidentally glance up and see who else is at the Lord's table. A good-looking person may distract an observer of the opposite sex. The sight of someone you cannot stand could disturb you. (In which case, why were you not reconciled before this hour? Seeing the person is a reminder of ongoing work for you!) We could turn this around: Seeing and being seen is a very useful exercise, since bodily movement to the Table is an announcement of intentions. Not "Look at me, folks, how pious I am for being here!" The day when attending church gave you status is long past. Instead, "Look at me, folks, as I look at you. We are sinners, but we are participants in the body and blood of Jesus Christ. We get to see what prophets and kings wanted to see but could not. We are part of the New Creation. Our bodies are on the line. We are committed."

A congregation is a gathering of people who bear one another's burdens. They are people who can support one another in illness and weakness, encourage one another when a task is heavy, speak a word of serious concern when they detect a lapse, and rejoice together in victories. Bodily presence at the Lord's Supper is not to be shunned but celebrated. Jesus Christ is here in a bodily presence with the bread. Why should you lower your eyes? Jesus Christ is here also as a bodily presence in you and your fellow members, who are to be Christs to each other. You should not lower your eyes. Look up.

And as you look up, you see that the last communicants are leaving the Table. One or another of these reflections took control of your mind. You have to scoop up a hymnal, a worship folder, and some leftover thoughts, since the service will come rather abruptly to its end.

5. "In the Morning . . ."

THE COMMUNION BEING ENDED, and your reflections too, the ministers clear the table and replace the cup and plate while you join in singing the CANTICLE, a short hymn of thanks. The minister offers a PRAYER, pronounces a BLESSING on you and all the people, and says, "Go in peace. Serve the Lord." (This used to be: "*Ita missa est*"—"the mass is ended; go in peace." Hence the term *mass*.) So you go in peace. You glance at your watch, wondering whether the service was over-long, given the rather large communing congregation today. A secular thought crowds in. I've got to catch Harry and Marge to see about our get-together on Friday. Will that weak battery start the motor? Has the roast burned? Such thoughts were not completely out of mind during the service. They are with you yet. But God is present among people whose minds wander, whose attentions stray, whose staying-power is short. He is present in a sanctuary that never quite leaves behind its world. God is also present in a world that should become a sanctuary. His space goes with you into that world.

You greet the ministers at the door, as you did back when they passed the peace of Christ, you chat with some friends, the car does start, the roast is only slightly burned, and most of the day is still ahead of you. By evening you will have passed through some of the usual cycles of boredom, drift, anger, and frustration. You hollered at the children. You grumbled about having to go to work tomorrow. You regretted your choice of an evening television show. You were not above conniving about how to get an advance on someone else. But you are no longer in the business of counting your sins on an adding machine, keeping score of them in a book, and dwelling on them. You do not think of this morning's

Communion as a way of wiping that slate clean only until the next Communion, depending upon how successful you were at confessing each of those sins. Instead, your whole way of life is part of the risen life.

When temptation comes or God seems remote, you know you can insist, "I am baptized! God, you promised . . ." When pride threatens and you want to make a claim upon God, you recall how this morning you knelt for the Lord's Supper, and how, in Jesus, God condescended to take on human form, to come under the low beams of your ceiling. Therefore your failure no longer leads to despair, nor your success to pride. Just as you are baptized and have heard the word, so now you have been at the table with God. You shared the family fellowship with Jesus Christ. You knew— and know—the presence and power of the Holy Spirit. You go in peace.

Tomorrow you will carry that presence, power, and peace with you. And if any of the the guilt of today remains to haunt, you make your appeal to the one who has said, "for you . . . for forgiveness of sins." You will wake spiritu- ally refreshed. It may be a blue-gray Monday, but as one who is baptized and has communed, you know how to start it: "In the morning, when you rise, make the sign of the corss and say, 'In the name of God, the Father, the Son, and the Holy Spirit. Amen.'" And you will confidently turn the day over to this God, who will work through you, according to the promise.

Questions for
Reflection and Discussion

THE QUESTIONS ON THE FOLLOWING PAGES may serve to deepen your reading of *The Lord's Supper* and apply the teaching to your life. If you are part of a study group, you may wish to read and discuss one chapter a week. Do not feel that you have to discuss each question. Choose those that are most important to the group. If the group is large, you might try breaking into twos or threes for discussion. You may wish to close your study session by singing a favorite Communion hymn or with prayer. At the conclusion of your discussion of *The Lord's Supper*, the group may choose to celebrate Holy Communion together.

Chapter 1. "For You . . . for Forgiveness"

1. What are your earliest memories of Holy Communion?

2. How has your experience of the Lord's Supper changed since then?

3. How important is it to you to celebrate the Lord's Supper in a way that is close to the original celebration of Christ and his disciples or the practice of the early Church?

4. In what ways do you want your celebration of Holy Communion to "tell you about you"?

5. At this point in your life, what does Holy Communion mean to you?

Chapter 2. Preparation

1. How do you prepare for your celebrations of Holy Communion?

2. In what ways might you better prepare yourself?

3. How frequently do you participate in Holy Communion? How do you feel about that?

4. How often do you think your congregation should celebrate Holy Communion? Why?

5. Think of the way your congregation celebrates Holy Communion. What features of this celebration are most important to you?

   In what ways would you like to see this service changed? Why?

6. In what ways are meals important occasions in your life?

7. How would you answer the question, "Why do Christians congregate once a week?"

Chapter 3. The Service

1. What part do stories play in your day-to-day life?

2. How can words or stories offer us forgiveness of sins, life, and salvation?

3. What, for you, is a good church service?

4. How do you understand the relationship between preaching and the Lord's Supper?

5. What is the role of faith in the celebration of the Lord's Supper?

6. How do you understand the relationship between the corporate and the personal dimension in believing? How do you understand the role of the "we" and the "I"?

7. How important are the historic creeds in your life and worship?

8. What do you think your response to Holy Communion should be?

Chapter 4. Reflections during Communion

1. How would you answer these questions: "What am I supposed to feel in Holy Communion?" and "Am I supposed to feel?"

2. What are the characteristics of "the sick soul"?
   The "healthy-minded" soul?
   In what category would you put yourself?

3. In what ways is forgiveness of sins important you you?

4. What were you taught about the presence of Christ in the sacrament? What do you believe now?

5. "No one should go away from the Lord's Supper unchanged." How do you understand this statement? Do you agree or disagree? Why?

6. How might you use Holy Communion as an occasion to reflect on your personal commitments?

7. In Martin Marty's view, what are the characteristics of a Christian congregation? How are these characteristics evident in your congregation?

Chapter 5. "In the Morning . . ."

1. What does Holy Communion have to do with your daily life?

   As a family member?

   As a friend?

   In your work?

   As a member of your community?

2. How might you remind yourself of the meaning of your participation in Holy Communion during the week?

3. How has your thinking about Holy Communion changed as a result of reading this book?

4. Which ideas did you find most helpful?

5. What questions do you still have?